NATIONAL GEOGRAPHIC KiDS

Surprising Stories Behind

EVERYDAY STUFF

STEPHANIE **WARREN DRIMMER**

NATIONAL GEOGRAPHIC
Washington, D.C.

TABLE OF **Contents**

LOOKS CHOCK-FOAL

Did you know that the **Slinky** was invented by **accident?** That the first **spatula** was used as a **surgical tool?** Or that **blue jeans** were originally worn by **gold miners?**

TAKE A LOOK AROUND YOU.

Ordinary objects you've probably never given a second thought, things like your sneakers, the refrigerator, or even a toothbrush, hold stories that might surprise you. Turns out, even the most familiar items and ideas can have totally unexpected origins.

Ketchup was once made from fish. Early lipsticks included ingredients like sheep sweat. Many modern sports come from shockingly violent pasts. And the evolution of acceptable bathroom habits? A truly horrifying history.

One thing is for sure: After reading this book, you won't see everyday stuff the same way again!

Toys & Games

Whether you're flying a kite or sending a Slinky down the stairs, it might seem like toys are just for playtime. But there's often a lot more to the story. Some toys began as tools of war or were banned for being bad influences. Others were invented by accident—or even inspired by aliens! All the items in this chapter have backgrounds that will surprise you. Ready to learn more? Game on!

FRISBEE

The Spectacular **Spinning Disk**

GO LONG!

Whoosh! It's a bird! It's a plane! It's an ancient Frisbee made of stone? Yikes—you'd better duck unless you want to lose your head!

The world's original disk-throwers were the ancient Greeks, who heaved weighty circles made of clay, stone, or metal at the world's first Olympic Games in 776 B.C. These disks didn't transform into the fun fliers you know today until the 1940s. At the time, some stressed-out college students were looking for a way to blow off steam. They started tossing the nearest thing laying around, which happened to be empty pie tins from the nearby William R. Frisbie bakery in Bridgeport, Connecticut, U.S.A. Sound familiar?

At about the same time, America was preoccupied with another kind of flying object: the UFO. In 1947, a man claimed that he'd spotted nine crescent-shaped ships speeding through the skies near Mount Rainier in Washington State, U.S.A. Wanting to capitalize on the craze, an inventor named Walter Frederick Morrison created a plastic toy meant to mimic a UFO's hovering flight.

Sales of the toy were slow until the president of the manufacturing company

AHEM, I WAS TOLD THERE WOULD BE **PIE ...**

started handing them out to East Coast college students. He was amazed to find that they were already throwing their own pie-tin "frisbies," and by 1957 the product had a new name. Today, more than 200 million Frisbees have been sold.

Bet You **Didn't Know**

One of the Frisbee's early names was Pluto Platter.

11

On a perfect windy day, what could be better than grabbing your kite, running as fast as you can, and seeing it suddenly soar into the air? Like magic, the wind catches it and tugs it skyward until it's just a colorful dot dancing on the breeze. But kites didn't start out as toys. Originally, they were tools of war.

HOW SHOCKING!

The first kites took to the skies above China around 1000 B.C., when armies used kite colors, patterns, and even flight maneuvers to signal to each other across long distances. The Chinese military even built bamboo-and-paper kites strong enough to carry humans. The idea was to ride them into the air to spy on enemy troops. According to 13th-century explorer Marco Polo, finding volunteers was tough: These kite-riders were prisoners who were forced to fly.

Around A.D. 700, Buddhist missionaries brought kites to Japan, where they were used for the popular sport of kite fighting: Opponents would coat their kite strings with ground glass or broken pottery, then swoop their kites through the air, trying to slice each other's strings.

The most famous flier in U.S. history is probably author, inventor, and American Founding Father Benjamin Franklin. In 1752, he sent a kite soaring into a thunderstorm with a metal key tied to the string to prove that lightning was electric in nature. When Franklin touched the key and felt a small zap, he proved his theory true. Talk about a shocking discovery!

Bet You Didn't Know

In England in 1822, a schoolteacher and inventor named George Pocock used a pair of kites to pull a carriage at 20 miles an hour (32 km/h).

I'LL GIVE IT A WHIRL!

HULA-HOOP

Spin **Cycle**

The modern Hula-Hoop exploded onto the scene in 1958, courtesy of the Wham-O toy company. Within just a few months, 25 million fans were spinning the plastic circles around their waists, arms, and necks. But they weren't the first to go crazy for the idea: People have been playing with hoop toys for thousands of years.

As long ago as 3000 B.C., the ancient Egyptians were bending reeds into circles, then swinging them around their waists, rolling them along the ground, and flinging them into the air. The Greeks caught on and made their own hoops out of grape-vines. But they didn't use them as toys. Instead, they were exercise equipment for those whose togas had gotten a little tight.

In the chilly Arctic, the indigenous Inuit people of North America and Greenland used hoops for target practice. Children would roll a hoop on the ground and then try to throw a pole through it to hone their harpooning skills. Native Americans improved their aim the same way. Members of one tribe, the Lakota, also used them for performing a hoop dance, spinning as many as 30 hoops on their bodies at once.

By the 14th century, hoops had whirled their way to England, where people of all ages went wild for the circles. Only one group wasn't a fan: British doctors, who blamed hoops for all kinds of ailments, from dislocated backs to heart attacks. But that didn't stop people from hooping: The toys are still popular today.

ALOHA 'OE

What's in **a Name?**

The name Hula-Hoop originated in the early 1800s, when British sailors traveled to the Hawaiian Islands and saw Polynesian women swaying their hips in the hula dance. The movement reminded them of the way their hips moved when playing with their hoop toys back home.

15

MARBLES

Having **a Ball**

No one knows exactly when or where marbles were invented, but one thing is for sure: They're very old. They've been discovered in prehistoric caves, buried in the ashes of Pompeii, and tucked away in the tombs of ancient Egyptians.

Today, marbles are toys, but archaeologists think ancient people used them to tell each other's fortunes. The earliest marbles were natural objects, such as stones that had been polished by running water. Celtic, Saxon, and African tribes used olives, chestnuts, hazelnuts, and fruit pits as marbles. In western Asia, people carved them from the knucklebones of dogs and sheep.

Kids changed marbles from tools of prophecy to playthings. Rounded semi-precious stones were found buried with an Egyptian child from around 3000 B.C. Experts think they're the earliest toy marbles ever discovered. American settlers also spotted Native American kids shooting marbles.

It wasn't until 1884 that someone came up with a way to mass-produce them. Sam Dyke of Akron, Ohio, U.S.A., invented a wooden box with six grooves, each holding a lump of clay. By rolling a wooden paddle back and forth over all the clay, a worker could create six marbles at once. The factory made about one million marbles every day. When a machine that could shape molten glass into a sphere was invented in 1915, glass marbles became a phenomenon.

YOU WILL HAVE PIZZA FOR LUNCH ...

What's in **a Name?**

The phrase "to knuckle down" likely comes from 17th-century England, where marble players often balanced on their knuckles while shooting marbles.

TEDDY **BEAR**

CAN WE JUST **HUG IT OUT?**

Cuddly, huggable teddy bears have been a classic kid's toy for more than a hundred years. But the stuffed animal got a strange start— on a 1902 hunting trip taken by U.S. president Theodore Roosevelt.

With a group of trappers, horses, tents, and 50 hunting dogs, Roosevelt set off for the Mississippi River swamps to bag a bear—a popular activity in those days. When a day passed with no bear sightings, Roosevelt's hosts got worried. To make sure the president wouldn't leave empty-handed, they caught a bear for him and tied it to a tree. But Roosevelt refused to shoot, saying it would have been unfair to the bear.

The story of the president's sportsmanship spread, and a cartoon of the incident was printed in the *Washington Post*. When candy store owner (and part-time toymaker) Morris Michtom saw the cartoon, he got an idea. He created a bear shape with some velvet, stuffed it, sewed on two eyes, and stuck it in his store window in Brooklyn, New York, U.S.A. Customers swarmed the store, begging for more of what came to be called "Teddy's bears."

The bears were so popular during the 1904 presidential election that Roosevelt adopted them as the symbol of his political party. Michtom went on to manufacture the toys, and made a fortune off his idea. Today, one of the very first teddy bears ever made is on display at the National Museum of American History in Washington, D.C.

Bet You **Didn't Know**

The world's largest teddy bear is 55 feet 4 inches (16.86 m) tall.

ONE OF MICHTOM'S EARLY TEDDY BEARS

THE BIGGEST Toy Fads

From rocks in a box to beanbag animals, it's sometimes surprising what toys become hits. They can cause store sellouts, high-priced online auctions, and even riots. Here are some fad must-haves that have topped kids' wish lists over the past 60 years. Is one of your all-time favorites—or your parent's—on the list?

1975
Pet Rocks

Too busy to walk a dog? No problem: Adopt a pet rock. A man named Gary Dahl came up with the idea after listening to his friends complain about the time it took to care for their living pets. Dahl sold 1.5 million rocks in a box for four dollars each; it made him a millionaire. Now that was a rock-solid idea.

1980
Rubik's Cube

When 29-year-old Hungarian professor Erno Rubik came up with his famously challenging cube, even *he* couldn't solve it. An instant sensation in the United States, it was launched at a Hollywood party hosted by actress Zsa Zsa Gabor. People were so obsessed with cracking the cube that the fad launched a wave of self-help books with titles like *How to Live With a Cubaholic*.

JUST ROLL WITH IT.

1995
Beanie Babies

Toy salesman Ty Warner wanted to create a collectible that kids could buy with their own money. He created animal-shaped beanbags that sold for just five dollars each, but he used clever marketing to create buzz. The toys were sold only at small shops, making them hard to find, and certain animals were "retired" without warning, which increased demand. It worked: Three years after they were introduced, Warner had sold more than 100 million Beanie Babies.

1975 **1980** **1985** **1990** **1995**

ME LOVE YOU!

1998
Furby

With its owl-like eyes and hamster-like body, this robotic pet was the must-have toy of the 1998 holiday season. Out of the box, it spoke the made-up language Furbish. As Furby spent more time with its owner, it would gradually learn English. Furbys flew off the shelves and sold for three times their sale price online.

2016
Hatchimals

Yet another interactive stuffed animal, the blockbuster Hatchimals—which came in different "species" like Pengualas and Burtles—arrived inside a speckled egg the size of a grapefruit, and pecked their way out. Hatchimals disappeared from stores almost the moment they were placed on shelves.

2000   2005   2010   2015   2020

2006
Nintendo Wii

A whole new kind of video gaming system, the Wii, got players up off the couch to play virtual sports like tennis and bowling using a motion-sensitive controller. Designed for the whole family, not just kids, Wii was a big hit. More than 10 million had been sold by the end of 2008. But the novelty wore off, and three years later, players had moved on to the next new system.

SLINKY

Most toys are popular for a short time and then fade away, never to be seen on store shelves again. But that's not true for the Slinky. Even though it's nothing more than a big spring (which often ends up tangled in a big knot), this toy has fascinated kids since a clumsy mistake led to its creation.

In 1943, mechanical engineer Richard James was experimenting with delicate springs to prevent fragile ship instruments from being tossed around in rough seas. When he accidentally knocked one of his prototypes off a shelf, James watched in amazement as the spring "walked" down a stack of books, onto a table, then to the floor.

James came home that evening jiggling with excitement. His wife, Betty, searched the dictionary to find the perfect name, landing on "Slinky." James designed a machine that could coil 80 feet (24 m) of wire into a spiral. The couple borrowed $500 and manufactured the first Slinkys.

Sales were slow until Christmas of 1945, when Gimbels department store in Philadelphia, Pennsylvania, U.S.A., agreed to let James demonstrate a Slinky for a crowd. Within minutes, he had sold 400. Since then, Slinkys have been used in physics classes, as radio antennas, and even in space, where astronauts used them to test the effects of zero gravity on springs. In 70 years on the market, more than 300 million have been sold.

ASTRONAUTS ON THE SPACE SHUTTLE *DISCOVERY* WITH A SLINKY IN 1985

Bet You **Didn't Know**

The song in the Slinky's TV advertisements is the longest-running jingle in the history of television advertising.

23

With its flashing lights, jangling sound effects, and the *thwack, thwack* of the flippers, pinball seems pretty harmless. So you might be surprised to learn the arcade game has been banned, shoved underground, and become a symbol of rebellion.

The forerunner of pinball was a European lawn game that had players rolling balls into holes on the ground. The game moved indoors in the 19th century, with the creation of a tabletop version called bagatelle. Players would shoot balls up an incline, then watch them roll down, bounce off pins, and land in pockets to score.

Across the pond in 1933, American victims of the Great Depression were out of work—and cash. They needed inexpensive entertainment, so the invention of the electric pinball machine was a hole in one. But the original pinball game didn't include a flipper (that was added in 1947), so players couldn't control the ball mid-play. That made pinball a game of chance, not skill. Some cities viewed it as a form of gambling. It didn't help pinball's reputation that the game had ties to organized crime—many machines belonged to the Mafia. Churches and schools argued that pinball was corrupting America's youth. In New York City, officials raided arcades, smashed the machines up with sledgehammers, and dumped them in the city's rivers.

Pinball remained illegal in most cities until the 1970s, when the ban was finally over-turned in major cities. But the game had been underground for so long that it became a symbol of rebellion and resistance. Movies and TV shows in the period often depicted teen rebels in arcades—*gasp!*—playing pinball.

Bet You **Didn't Know**

It's still illegal to play pinball on Sundays in Ocean City, New Jersey, U.S.A.

STEP AWAY FROM THE GAME ...

CHESS

Game of **War**

Chess didn't start as a game. It was a tool meant to train military leaders in the art of battle. The two sides represented opposing armies, and the first player to capture the opponent's king was the winner.

Almost 1,500 years ago, people in India were playing an ancient version of chess called *chaturanga*, which means "the four divisions." The name refers to the four parts of an ancient Indian army: the foot soldiers, the horses, the chariots, and the elephants trained for combat. When traders carried the game out of India in their packs, new cultures adopted chaturanga as their own. Many modern chess terms have origins from Persia: When the king was attacked, the player would say *"Shah"* (*shah* means "king"). That eventually became "Check." And when the king was surrounded and the game won, the winning player would shout *"Shah mat!*—The king is trapped!" That became "Checkmate!"

OOH, GOOD MOVE!

By A.D. 1000, chess had spread throughout Europe. Chariot pieces became castles and elephants became bishops. The queen got the biggest makeover: What started as a male counselor to the king and the weakest piece on the board became a female piece and the most powerful in the game.

Chess was a big hit with European nobility, who used it to practice military strategy, and it became known as the Royal Game. Today, 15 centuries after it was invented, more books have been written about chess than about any other game or sport in the world.

I'M **COMING** FOR YOU, KING!

Bet You **Didn't Know**

The world's youngest chess grandmaster is Sergey Karjakin, who lives in Russia. He earned the title at 12 years old.

PAC-MAN

A **Pizza** Pop Culture

Chomp, chomp, chomp! As you maneuver the yellow mouth around the maze, evading ghosts and gobbling up dots, you're playing the most successful arcade game in history: Pac-Man.

Twenty-seven-year-old Toru Iwatani was reaching for a slice of pizza in 1979 when he stopped short. He noticed that the pie, which was missing two slices, looked like a mouth. Iwatani worked for the Japanese video game company Namco and came up with the idea of a game all about eating.

At the time, people thought of arcades as dark, dirty places where teenagers gathered to play violent games involving aliens or soldiers. Iwatani wanted to change the perception by creating a game that had a wider appeal. So he turned the shape he saw in the pizza into a hungry yellow mouth on the run from evil ghosts. He kept the rules easy and the controls simple. In 1980, Pac-Man was born.

The game was released in Japan as Pakku-Man, after the Japanese word for the sound of a mouth opening and closing. It wasn't a big success. But when it hit the United States with a new, shorter name, everything changed. Kids lined up for a chance to spend their quarters guiding the chomping mouth around the screen. The game was so popular that it inspired 16 spin-offs, including Ms. Pac-Man. By the 1990s, it had earned about $2.5 billion. That's a lot of quarters!

MS. PAC-MAN TV GAME

CHAPTER 1 • Toys & Games

YOU SEEIN' WHAT I'M SEEIN'?

Bet You Didn't Know

One neighborhood in Seattle, Washington, U.S.A., has a pavement park painted like a life-size Pac-Man game.

29

A PIECE OF **History**

GAME ON!

When Monopoly first became popular in the 1930s, it didn't come with pieces. Charles Darrow, who didn't invent the game but did sell it to Parker Brothers and made it a commercial success, assumed players would use items from around the house, like a stray button or a penny. The first metal tokens were introduced in the mid-1930s, and now some might say choosing which piece to use is an important part of the game.

Old Shoe

An original piece, the beat-up boot is based on those laborers would have worn in the 1930s. Like some other tokens, including the thimble, the wheelbarrow, and the iron, the old shoe is said to symbolize hard work, and the wealth that can come from it.

Top Hat

Another original metal Monopoly token, the top hat was meant to represent the game's lead character, Mr. Monopoly, who was pictured on the box of an early edition dressed to the nines. Also known as Rich Uncle Pennybags, some speculate that Mr. Monopoly was meant to represent American business tycoon J. P. Morgan.

Race Car

Today, the car is the most popular token (after all, it seems most at home on Park Place). But the race car wasn't part of the game until 1936. It's said to be based on the car Mr. Monopoly would have driven around the streets of Atlantic City, New Jersey, U.S.A., which the game is based on.

Cat

In February 2013, Monopoly got an update. Fans were invited to vote for which old token would go to "jail for life" and what its replacement would be. The iron was voted out, and a cat was added—beating out a robot, guitar, helicopter, and diamond ring.

WHICH WAY TO **JURASSIC PARK PLACE?**

T. rex

In 2017, Monopoly once again sought to update its tokens. More than 4.3 million online votes from around the world were tallied. The result was a major token overhaul: The boot, the wheelbarrow, and the thimble were retired to make room for a penguin, a ducky, and, most popular of all, a roaring T. rex.

CHAPTER 2
Food

When you unwrap your sandwich at lunchtime, you're probably not expecting any surprises. But some foods have unbelievable histories, whether they make your tummy rumble or gross you out. Are there secrets hiding in that peanut butter sandwich? Or concealed inside that chocolate treat? Here are some food stories to sink your teeth into!

PEANUT
BUTTER

There's no denying it: Americans love peanut butter. A whopping 94 percent of U.S. homes have a jar. But the familiar snack food is actually sticky with secrets.

It's strange but true: Peanut butter doesn't contain nuts at all. Peanuts are legumes, in the same family as beans and peas. And while many history books credit famous African-American scientist George Washington Carver as peanut butter's inventor, that's not quite right.

Carver was one of America's most ingenious inventors, and he did come up with more than 300 uses for peanuts, including as an ingredient in shampoo, shaving cream, and glue. But he didn't dream up peanut butter. The ancient Aztec were responsible for the sticky-sweet substance—they were roasting and mashing peanuts into a paste thousands of years ago. Centuries afterward, several inventors came up with processes for roasting, smashing, and preserving peanut

GEORGE WASHINGTON CARVER

butter, including a man named Harvey Kellogg—the doctor better known as the mastermind behind Kellogg's cereal.

In 1895, Kellogg promoted peanut butter as a promising food for his older patients who had poor teeth and couldn't chew tougher proteins, like meat. Around the same time, Carver encouraged southern farmers to plant peanuts instead of cotton. When peanut butter was presented at the 1904 World's Fair in St. Louis, Missouri, U.S.A., its popularity skyrocketed. Americans haven't stopped scooping and spreading the stuff ever since.

Bet You **Didn't Know**

The average American eats 1,500 peanut butter and jelly sandwiches before graduating from high school.

KETCHUP

A **Fishy** Past

DON'T YOU **NEED ME?**

It's America's favorite condiment: 97 percent of U.S. kitchens have a bottle of tomato ketchup stowed in the fridge. But its origins are anything but American. The word "ketchup" comes from the Chinese *ki-tsiap*, the name of a sauce made out of fermented fish, or broken down chemically—and containing no tomatoes at all.

Sailors visiting Southeast Asia were probably the first foreigners to encounter ki-tsiap. When they came home, they tried to reproduce it using ingredients they had on hand, like walnuts, celery, oysters, and anchovies. *Ewww!* They used their concoctions as flavor boosters for soups and sauces.

Though the Aztec had been growing tomatoes in North America since about A.D. 700, ketchup wouldn't get its most familiar ingredient until the early 1800s.

Many people steered clear of tomatoes for centuries, believing they were poisonous. Not scientist James Mease from Philadelphia, Pennsylvania, U.S.A., who created the first tomato ketchup in 1812. He was such a fan that his original recipe referred to them as "love apples"—an old French nickname.

36

Before tomatoes were added, ketchup was really hard to store. It often contained bacteria, yeast, and molds that made it dangerous to eat. But a man named Henry J. Heinz from Pittsburgh, Pennsylvania, realized that adding tomatoes—which contain high amounts of the natural preservative pectin—allowed the sauce to stay safely on the shelf. Today, the Kraft Heinz Company sells more than 650 million bottles a year.

Bet You **Didn't Know**

Heinz ketchup's red color originally came from coal tar.

GUYS, YOU FORGOT THE BEST **INGREDIENT.**

WEIRD Food Trends

If you think your best friend's smelly tuna sandwich is a strange lunch choice, check out this list. At one point in the past, these odd foods were the height of cool. Would you try them?

1920s
Fruit Cocktail

Before the 1920s, raw oysters had been a common appetizer. But then, a new predinner treat hit tables: fruit cocktail, bowls of diced melon and grapes that had been sprinkled with powdered sugar and decorated with marshmallows.

1940s
SPAM

When the United States entered World War II, the Army had to figure out how to feed its soldiers overseas. Regular meat would spoil on the long journey, so the Army turned to a canned meat product called SPAM: mashed-up pork and potato starch with seasonings and preservatives. To date, well over seven billion cans of SPAM have been sold worldwide.

1920	1930	1940	1950	1960

1930s
Jell-O Salad

Today we think of it as a dessert, but wiggly, jiggly Jell-O often used to be filled with ingredients like chicken, hard-boiled eggs, and grated carrots. Cold Jell-O molds were all the rage in the Depression era. Popular recipes included Cottage Cheese and Salmon Mold and lemon-flavored Ring Around the Tuna.

Delicious with Breakfast
Delicioso con el desayuno

TANG

ORANGE NARANJA
NATURAL FLAVOR WITH OTHER NATURAL FLAVOR
SABOR NATURAL CON OTRO SABOR NATURAL

100% Daily Value of
Vitamin C
and a Good Source of
Calcium
100% de su Vitamina C Diaria
y Buena Fuente de Calcio

MAKES **6** QUARTS
RINDE CUARTOS

NET WT • PESO NETO 20 OZ (1 LB 4 OZ) 566g

DRINK MIX • BEBIDA INSTANTÁNEA

I'M OUT OF **THIS WORLD!**

1960s
Instant Food

Astronaut John Glenn was the first person to sip Tang, a just-add-water powdered orange drink, when he orbited Earth for the first time in 1962. He used it to mask the funky taste of his spaceship's drinking water, but on Earth people quickly became obsessed with Tang and all other astronaut-inspired foods. Instant mashed potatoes, squeezable cheese, and whipped cream in a can were this decade's staples.

1970 — 1980 — 1990 — 2000 — 2010

1990s
Fat Free

Dieters everywhere rejoiced when Frito-Lay released potato chips in 1998 boasting "All the Taste 1 Gram of Fat." People loved the idea that scientists had removed the unhealthy parts of their favorite snacks. But the claim was too good to be true. Frito-Lay's secret fat-free ingredient, Olestra, wound up sending people running to the bathroom when they ate too much of it. *Whoops!*

2010s
Bacon Everything

Salty, smoky bacon is the ideal topping for a burger or side to eggs and hash browns, and it's been popular for a long time. But in the 2010s, chefs went bacon-crazy, using it in everything from doughnuts to soda. In 2012, Burger King even released a bacon-topped ice-cream sundae.

39

SODA

Bubble **Trouble**

Today, soda's reputation is on the rocks—it's been banned from schools and accused of being bad for your health. Yet it's still guzzled in every country and available in every flavor imaginable, from lemon-lime to bubble gum. It might be hard to believe, but soda started out as a health product.

People have been downing mineral waters that bubble up from natural sources for hundreds of years. They thought that drinking or bathing in natural mineral water could cure all kinds of illnesses, from gallstones to scurvy.

GOT SCURVY? **SAY NO MORE.**

Smart sellers started mixing flavorings into mineral water to make it taste better. They opened soda fountains that became a place for people to sip, sit, and socialize. To entice a crowd, these soda shops were decorated with marble counters and brass dispensers. Servers whipped up "medicinal" concoctions that included flavors still popular today, like ginger ale and root beer. Carbonation was added around 1832 to give the drinks a fashionable fizz. Dr. Pepper, the oldest major soft drink in America, was marketed in 1885 as an energy drink and "brain tonic."

Soon, people wanted to carry their "health" drinks on the go. But inventors had trouble figuring out how to keep the bubbles inside the bottle. More than 1,500 patents for corks, tops, and lids were filed before the soda industry hit on the crimped metal cap that can still be found on glass bottles today. Soda's popularity isn't likely to fizzle out anytime soon.

I'M SURE I WAS A **FAN FAVORITE ...**

Bet You **Didn't Know**

Soda companies have made drinks in flavors including turkey and gravy, yogurt, and brussels sprouts.

41

POPCORN

A **Kernel** of Truth

WE CAN'T HANDLE THE **PRESSURE!**

Who could stop at eating just a handful of satisfying, crunchy popcorn? Popcorn pops when water and air trapped inside a corn kernel's hard outer shell heats up, turns into steam, and expands. When enough pressure builds up, *POP!* The starches and proteins in the inner part of the kernel expand into fluffy white flakes. Today, we add a little butter and salt to make it a tasty snack.

ADMIT ONE
834283
834283

Bet You **Didn't Know**

The first commercial popcorn machine, invented in 1885, was a cart with a gasoline burner. Vendors used to park wherever crowds gathered, including movie theaters—which is how popcorn became known as a movie snack.

Turns out, people have been shoveling versions of popcorn into their mouths for a long time. In 2012, archaeologists discovered 6,700-year-old ears of corn on the northern coast of Peru—and they could tell the kernels had been popped.

The ancient wild ancestor of corn, called teosinte, has been cultivated for about 9,000 years. Teosinte looks almost nothing like corn. It has just a few kernels per stalk, and they're too hard to eat or grind into flour. But teosinte can be popped, and experts believe that was the first way ancient people ate corn.

In North America, the Iroquois people popped corn kernels in jars filled with heated sand. When the colonists moved in, they adopted the snack, eating it with milk and sugar like a breakfast cereal, or coated with molasses, like today's kettle corn. By the 1800s, popcorn was one of the most popular snack foods, and it still is: Today, Americans eat about 17 billion quarts (16 billion L) of it every year.

TEOSINTE

HOT
DOGS

No More **Mystery Meat**

I AM NOT **AMUSED.**

What's in **a Name?**

According to legend, the name "hot dog" caught on when a concession worker at a 1902 New York Giants baseball game enticed customers to buy his "dachshund sausages" by yelling, "Get 'em while they're hot!"

COME AND **GET IT!**

They're an iconic American food, a staple of state fairs and the Fourth of July. But did you know the humble hot dog has a royal history?

Historians believe the hot dog got its start in ancient Rome when the emperor's cook, Gaius, discovered that stuffed pig intestines puffed up in the heat of an oven.

Much later, German sausage-makers in Frankfurt and Vienna disputed who slung dogs first (some still do). The people of Vienna (Wien in German) claim they came up with the original "wienerwurst." But folks in Frankfurt say *they* invented the "frankfurter."

The man responsible for making the hot dog an American obsession was Nathan Handwerker, a Polish immigrant who worked a hot dog stand in Coney Island, in Brooklyn, New York, U.S.A., in 1915. Though he made only $11 a week, he saved carefully, and when he had $300, he started his own stand and put his boss out of business. That was the beginning of Nathan's Famous, sponsor of the annual Fourth of July hot dog eating contest and now one of the world's best known hot dog brands.

In 1939, hot dogs returned to their royal roots when America's First Lady Eleanor Roosevelt served them to England's King George VI and his queen at a picnic. People worried that the Brits would pooh-pooh the modest meal, but the royals liked the dogs so much that the king had seconds.

SUSHI

Not-so-Fancy **Fish**

I'M A **GENIUS!**

Today, sushi lovers seek out the freshest fish they can find. But the original dish would have made these fine diners hold their noses: It was made with pungent, fermented fish!

Sushi's ancient origins are surrounded in myth and legend. One story says that a Japanese woman kept pots of rice in birds' nests. When she went back to collect her pots, fish scraps from the birds' meals had fallen into the rice. In the meantime, the rice had fermented and preserved the fish. The woman had accidentally become the world's first sushi chef.

While that tale is probably fiction, historians do know that between the third and fifth centuries B.C. in Southeast Asia, people were putting fish, salt, and rice in barrels and leaving them to ferment for an entire year. After 12 months of waiting, they'd scrape away the rice and eat the (definitely stinky) fish. And by the 19th century, street vendors in Tokyo, Japan, had switched from a long fermentation to a quick cure, and sold the fish over vinegar-spiked rice to hungry workers.

The modern version of sushi developed in the 20th century, when refrigeration made it possible to safely eat uncooked fish and fish. Raw fish over rice became a worldwide sensation, and it is now available everywhere, from fancy restaurants to grocery stores.

Bet You **Didn't Know**

People in parts of Yunan, China, and northern Thailand still prepare sushi the original way—fermenting fish in barrels with rice.

PICKLES

The **Sweet-and-Sour** Truth

When you hear the word "pickle," you probably think of the sour, crunchy cucumber spears that sit next to your burger. But nearly anything can be pickled, from a green bean to a side of beef.

Pickling is a process that involves pouring a salty solution called brine over food. Given time, tiny microbes develop and begin eating the sugars in the food and converting them to acid. The bacteria that cause food to rot can't survive in an acidic environment, which means pickled foods are less likely to spoil. In the days before refrigeration, pickling was a necessity. Everyone, from sailors on months-long voyages at sea to families surviving long winters, ate pickled food when fresh wasn't available.

Nearly every culture on Earth has its own pickling traditions. The English make sweet cucumber pickles with vinegar, sugar, and spices. The French make tiny, spiced whole cucumbers called cornichons.

CORNICHON

OUI, PETITE AND **POWERFUL!**

Bet You **Didn't Know**

Though it's never been backed up by solid science, many athletes believe that drinking pickle juice helps them perform.

The Russians pickle tomatoes; the Japanese, plums; and Italians, eggplants. But perhaps the most familiar pickle of all is the kosher dill.

For the Eastern European Jewish community, barrels of pickled cucumbers, beets, and cabbage were a staple that livened up their winter diets. When they began immigrating to the United States at the turn of the 20th century, the Jews brought their kosher dill pickles with them. They sold pickles on pushcarts on the streets, especially in New York City. Today's best Jewish delis still serve spears of perfectly crunchy pickles alongside their mile-high sandwiches.

PIE

A **Sweet** Story

Whether their favorite is apple or pumpkin, chocolate or lemon meringue, many people love pie. And for some, the buttery, flaky crust is the best part. But for hundreds of years, the crust wasn't meant to be eaten: Instead, diners would crack it open and scoop out the insides.

Three thousand years ago, ancient Egyptians used bread dough to hold a mixture of nuts, honey, and fruits. But the first true pastry came from the ancient Greeks, who made a paste of flour and water, then wrapped it around meat before cooking. The crust was too tough to eat, but it was a perfect all-in-one baking dish, storage container, and serving vessel.

The Romans baked up their own version of pie, though their recipes might not sound so appetizing today. Guests at a Roman party might have eaten individual pies filled with eels or doves. As they conquered lands and built roads across

Bet You **Didn't Know**

In medieval England, pies were cooked in long narrow pans and were called coffins. *Creepy.*

their empire, the Romans took their handheld pastries along with them.

As time passed, cooks began to add lard or butter to their flour-and-water crusts, making a pastry that people could finally eat without breaking a tooth. Pies adorned the feast tables of medieval European kings. Sometimes they were for entertainment instead of eating. Small, live animals like rabbits, frogs, or birds would be hidden under a prebaked piecrust. When it was cut, the animals would burst out to dazzle the guests.

I'M GETTING OUT OF HERE!

FREEDOM!

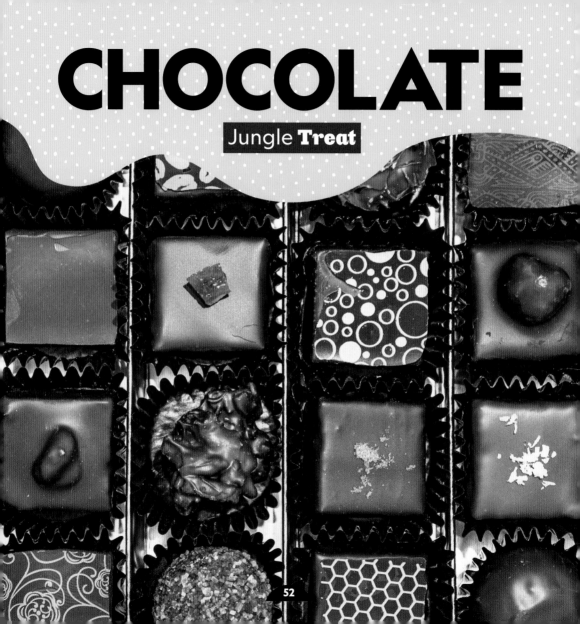

CHOCOLATE

Jungle **Treat**

I'VE **BEAN** TOLD I'M **MAGICAL** ...

Whether it's a piece of candy, a warm cookie, or a gooey brownie, you know anything made of chocolate is going to be smooth and sweet on your tongue. But did you know this favorite dessert treat comes from a rain forest plant?

Deep in the jungles of Central and South America, strange-looking trees grow with foot-long pink-and-yellow pods clinging to their trunks and branches. Inside these freaky fruit pods are cacao beans. In their natural state, cacao beans are bitter. But that didn't stop the ancient Maya and Aztec peoples from enjoying them 4,000 years ago. They ground the beans into cocoa powder and mixed it with water, vanilla, honey, and chili peppers to create a bitter, spicy beverage, called *chocolatl*. Believed to have magical properties, only rulers, warriors, priests, and nobles were allowed to drink it. And it was often used as an offering to the gods.

When Spanish conquistadores traveled to Mexico looking for gold and silver in the 16th century, many returned without precious metals but with ships full of cacao beans. Europeans mixed their cocoa powder with sugar instead of chilies, added milk, and started slurping up this chocolate drink by the gallon.

Two hundred years later, people figured out how to turn liquid chocolate into solid bars. By the American Revolutionary War, chocolate bars were so beloved that some soldiers received them as payment instead of money. Today, the average American eats half a pound (227 g) of chocolate every month.

Bet You **Didn't Know**

Food scientists use an exact mix of fats called triglycerides in their chocolate recipes to make sure the dessert melts in your mouth, not your hand.

USEFUL **Utensils**

The last time you scooped up your soup or sliced your steak, did you stop to think about where the utensils in your hands come from? Before they were an ordinary part of mealtime, they started out as dangerous weapons, scandalous accessories, and even poison-testers.

Spoon

The earliest spoons were objects found in nature, like seashells, gourds, and sections of bamboo. Ancient languages offer hints at which items were used: The Anglo-Saxon word *spon* means "a chip of wood." By the Middle Ages, royalty used spoons made from precious metals, giving rise to the phrase "born with a silver spoon in his mouth" to describe someone born into a wealthy family.

Forks

Originating in the Middle East, the fork spread to Europe when a princess from Byzantium (modern-day Istanbul) married a royal from Italy in the 11th century. Italians were scandalized when she—*gasp!*—speared her food with a two-tined, golden fork. That's because the Roman Catholic Church back then taught that people should only use the forks they had been born with: their fingers.

I'M UN-**FORK**-GETTABLE.

Chopsticks

About 5,000 years ago, the Chinese began using twigs from their cooking fires to pull hot morsels out of the pot. Over time, people traded twigs for chopsticks. During the era of the ancient Chinese dynasties, many used chopsticks made of silver, believing they would turn black if they touched poisoned food. While that's not true, silver can tarnish if it touches garlic or onions. That probably led to some mealtime misunderstandings!

STICK WITH ME.

Knife

It was customary during the Middle Ages in Europe for everyone to bring his or her own knife to dinner. That meant every person in the dining room had not only a utensil but also a weapon. Fights were common, and dinnertime became so dangerous that King Louis XIV of France banned pointed knives at the table in 1669.

KNIFE TO MEET YOU!

CHAPTER 3

Fashion

You might not know it, but when you throw on a favorite pair of jeans or slip on your sneakers, you're not just putting on clothes—you're wearing history. Long before they found a way into your closet, many of your outfits were influenced by cowboys, beach-goers, basketball stars, and even gold miners. Some of the clothes in your laundry basket were originally made for comfort; others for war. What's the story behind your go-to outfit?

BLUE
JEANS

One Tough **Trend**

These days, all kinds of people, from ranchers to CEOs, toddlers to teenagers, grandparents to movie stars, wear jeans. Denim is the world's most popular fabric. But how did that happen?

Blue jeans got their start by mistake. In the 18th century, craftspeople in Nîmes, France, tried to replicate a durable Italian fabric called serge. They didn't get it exactly right, so they named their new creation *serge de Nîmes.* Eventually, "serge" was dropped and the name shortened to "denim."

Denim might have stayed in France forever if not for the American gold rush. When gold was discovered at the base of the Sierra Nevada in 1848, hordes of hopeful miners showed up to strike it rich. As they slid through narrow mine shafts and scraped along rocks in search of treasure, they kept tearing their pants. Finally, Jacob Davis, a tailor in Reno, Nevada, U.S.A., teamed up with a German immigrant named Levi Strauss in 1871 to solve the problem. They started making sturdy denim pants reinforced with metal rivets: the very first Levi's.

Jeans were initially popular with people whose clothes took a beating, like farmers and laborers. Then celebrities including James Dean, Elvis, and Marilyn Monroe wore them in films in the 1950s and '60s, and the world went denim-crazy. Since then, cuts have ranged from bell-bottom to baggy to skinny, but blue jeans never seem to go out of style.

What's in a Name?
Jeans were originally called waist overalls.

JAMES DEAN

59

PAJAMAS

Nutty **Nightwear**

What's better than curling up in your coziest pair of pj's? Not much. But for a long time, people couldn't do that because they didn't wear pajamas at all. From ancient times until the 1800s, just about everyone either slept in their day clothes or stripped down to their undergarments.

From about the early 19th century until pajamas were invented, most European men wore loose, long garments called nightshirts to sleep. Women wore nightgowns, which were nearly identical to the men's nightshirts, just slightly longer. When morning came, no one changed. Instead, they all put their day clothes on over their nightwear—men tucking the long ends of their nightshirts into their pants.

In those days, most people owned very few garments. Wearing night-clothes under their day clothing provided a protective barrier between their nicer outfits and the dirt and sweat on their (often unbathed) skin. That meant people could wash their day clothing less often, which helped it last longer.

When washing machines were invented in the 1900s, people began to wear special outfits just for sleeping. British officers serving stints in India came home with "paejamas," loose trousers tied with a drawstring. By 1898, English merchants were selling them with matching shirts. At first, only men wore them. But by the 1920s, evening pajamas in satin or silk became the height of glamour for fashionable ladies lounging at home. Today, people cozy up in all kinds of nightwear, from flannel onesies to old camp T-shirts.

Bet You **Didn't Know**

Footed pajamas may have originated to protect the wearer from biting bugs. *Ouch!*

MY PLANS ARE **FOILED!**

BEDBUG

61

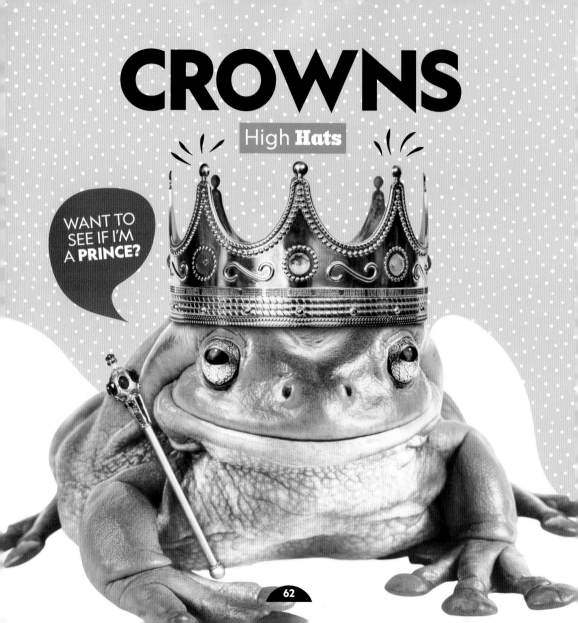

Crowns have visually set the rulers apart from the peasants since prehistoric times. The oldest crown ever discovered was found in a remote cave near the Dead Sea in modern-day Israel. It's made of blackened copper shaped into a band decorated with figures of vultures and doors. No one knows who wore this piece of historical headgear, but it's thought to be more than 6,000 years old.

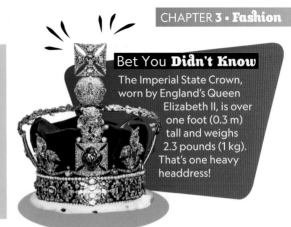

Bet You Didn't Know

The Imperial State Crown, worn by England's Queen Elizabeth II, is over one foot (0.3 m) tall and weighs 2.3 pounds (1 kg). That's one heavy headdress!

Throughout history, crowns have been designed to reflect or celebrate nature. In North America, indigenous tribal leaders adorned their headdresses with feathers from rare and beautiful birds. French emperor Napoleon wore a wreath of golden laurel leaves, a symbol of victory in ancient times. Cleopatra's crown was decorated with three cobras, representing royalty in ancient Egypt.

One of the oldest types of crown is the tiara. In ancient times, it was a tall, pointed hat made of leather or metal. Today, tiaras are bejeweled circlets that grace the heads of royals for fancy occasions—or anyone playing dress-up. Great Britain's Catherine, Duchess of Cambridge, famously donned a tiara at her 2011 wedding to Prince William. But her diamond-encrusted headpiece has nothing on her grandmother-in-law's: The Imperial State Crown, worn by Queen Elizabeth II, is bedecked with 273 pearls, 17 sapphires, 11 emeralds, 5 rubies, and 2,868 diamonds—one of which is the second largest diamond in the world at a whopping 317 carats. Now that's what we call a crown!

MY CROWN, C'EST **MAGNIFIQUE**, NON?

NAPOLEON

SNEAKERS

Fancy-Free **Footwear**

I AM BEACH READY!

Plimsolls became the trendy footwear of the mid-1800s. Different styles were released for different activities, until people were wearing these sneakerlike shoes for everything from playing lawn games to fighting wars. Explorer Robert F. Scott even took a pair with him on his journey to discover the South Pole.

Imagine going to the beach in the 19th century. No giant, plush towels or breezy beachwear in sight. And definitely no sand and surf between your toes: Your feet would be hidden away in a pair of sturdy leather boots.

Sound uncomfortable? Today, yes. But boots were normal footwear for the English middle and lower classes, who started flocking to the seaside once railroads made travel accessible to everyone. Seeing a need for a better beach shoe, in the 1830s the Liverpool Rubber Company developed a "plimsoll" with canvas sides and a rubber sole—the style still looks familiar today.

ROBERT F. SCOTT

In 1917, the Converse Rubber Shoe Company introduced the first basketball shoe, the All Star. To help sell the sneaker, they used a brilliant new marketing technique: hiring basketball players to act as brand ambassadors. The most famous endorsement deal ever came in 1984 when Nike signed a rookie named Michael Jordan. It was against the NBA's league rules, but Nike forked over the $5,000-per-game fine so Jordan could wear his namesake Air Jordans on the court anyway.

MICHAEL JORDAN

SHHH, I'M SNEAKING.

What's in **a Name?**

"Sneakers" refers to the nearly noiseless, rubber-padded footsteps of someone wearing the shoe.

CONVERSE
ALL STAR
Chuck Taylor

HIGH HEELS

STEP OFF, THERE'S A NEW HEEL IN TOWN!

Bet You **Didn't Know**

Cowboys wear high-heeled boots to keep their feet from slipping through the stirrups.

66

High-heeled shoes are considered a fashion staple by many women, and they've been around for centuries. But if you go back far enough in history, it wasn't women who were wearing them. It was men.

The first high heels were purely practical: Ancient Egyptian butchers wore them to keep their feet out of the blood that covered their floors. Later, medieval Europeans wore heels to keep their feet out of the slop that flowed through the filthy streets.

In 1533, Catherine de Medicis tottered into her wedding ceremony to France's Duke of Orleans wearing a pair of heels. She was hoping they would help her look more commanding and older than her 14 years. Soon, high heels were considered a fashion must for both men and women in high society. The trend got extreme: Venetian noblewomen wore a type of shoe called a chopine that could be more than two feet (0.6 m) high. They had to clutch four or five noblemen just to walk.

Perhaps the biggest fan of high heels was French king Louis XIV. Since he was just five feet four inches (1.6 m) tall, he liked that high heels added to his stature,

allowing him to look down on his subjects. Heels fell from their fashion heights during the French Revolution in 1789, when the last thing most people wanted was to resemble the hated nobility. But Victorian women started wearing them again in the 19th century, although men's footwear stayed flat on the ground. And it's mostly remained that way ever since.

I'VE GOT LEGS FOR DAYS!

KING LOUIS XIV

FUNKY **Fashion Fads**

Some were odd, some were uncomfortable, some were downright deadly. One thing is for sure: These strange fashion trends of the past will make you appreciate your T-shirts and hoodies.

1560s Ruffs

In the 16th century, men had been wearing undershirts with ruffles that spilled out over their shirt collars for decades. But over time, these "ruffs" got supersized. Eventually, ruffs were made with a whopping 18 feet (5.5 m) of fabric that was folded into 600 pleats and extended eight inches (20 cm) from the neck. They were so big that the nobles who wore them had to use special long utensils to eat.

1600s Powdered Wigs

For well over two centuries starting in the 1600s, the upper classes wore curled, white-powdered wigs. But you probably don't know why: Many of them were bald! Disease outbreaks resulted in hair loss and smelly, open sores on some victims' heads. To conceal their suffering scalps, people took to wearing wigs made of goat, horse, or human hair. To cover any odors, the wigs were powdered with scents like lavender and orange.

1550   1600   1650   1700   1750

1580s Blackened Teeth

During the Elizabethan era, sweet cookies and cakes were all the rage. But sugar was so expensive only the wealthy could afford it. The dessert craze combined with a lack of oral hygiene meant that many nobles' teeth turned black and fell out. Instead of causing embarrassment, rotting teeth became a trend—people with pearly whites would use cosmetics to blacken their smile on purpose.

PEARLY WHITES ARE SO 14TH CENTURY.

WARN ME IF IT GETS WINDY.

1850s
Crinolines

Victorian ladies were literal fashion victims. Not only did they have to squeeze into corsets, but they also wore huge hoops under their dresses. Made of horsehair, wood, or steel and measuring up to six feet (1.8 m) across, crinolines weren't just heavy and uncomfortable—they were sometimes deadly. Women got stuck in doorways, caught in carriage spokes, and were even blown off cliffs by gusts of wind.

1980s
Shoulder Pads

When women started entering the workforce in record numbers, they knew they needed to prove themselves in a world dominated by men. So fashion became all about power: Women's suit jackets (and just about every other top) included shoulder pads. Meant to create a strong, powerful look, some shoulder pads were so big they almost reached the wearer's ears. Big shoulders have come back in style since then. Time to raid Grandma's closet!

| 1800 | 1850 | 1900 | 1950 | 2000 |

1960s
Paper Dresses

Disposable items were all the rage in the 1960s. People loved tossing out their plates and forks after dinner—so why not their clothing? In 1966, the Scott Paper Company introduced the paper dress. It was meant to be a marketing gimmick, but the paper dresses became a huge fad. When they ripped, wearers patched them with a little tape, and when they got dirty they were simply thrown away.

ZIPPERS

A **Fasten-ating** Story

Zippers can be tricky—they get stuck, they refuse to catch, or, worst of all, you can forget to close them. But the zipper was invented to make getting dressed easier. Whitcomb Judson was the first to create a fastener, called the "clasp locker," which was meant to quickly fasten the tall, many-buttoned boots fashionable in the late 19th century. Unfortunately, his invention didn't work.

It wasn't until one of Judson's employees, Gideon Sundback, switched out the hook-and-eye system for a series of small interlocking teeth that the zipper as we know it was developed.

It was actually a flop at first. People were used to fastening long rows of buttons, and they had no interest in changing their ways. The first big buyer of zippers was the U.S. Army. Officials thought the clever closures would help aviators fasten their flight suits faster.

In 1923, the B.F. Goodrich company added zippers to galoshes—rubber covers that people wore over their shoes to protect them in bad weather. It's said that a Goodrich executive named the contraption when he slid the tab down the teeth and exclaimed, "Zip 'er up!"

Zippers glided from galoshes to children's clothing when they were advertised as a way for kids to dress themselves. Today, zippers are a feature in so many clothing items that we take them for granted. That is, until they get stuck!

ARMY PILOTS WERE SOME OF THE FIRST TO WEAR ZIPPERS.

Bet You **Didn't Know**

The first use of the word "zip," in 1875, was to describe the sound a mosquito makes.

POCKETS

Everything in **Its Place**

Bet You Didn't Know

One 19th-century woman's pockets were said to include a handkerchief, spare change, a diary, keys, a sewing kit, eyeglasses, bits of biscuit, nutmeg and a grater, a bottle of smelling salts, and an orange or apple.

Pockets aren't exactly the most exciting part of a piece of clothing. You might not even notice them—until your hands get cold or you need a place to put something.

NOW WHERE DID I PUT **THAT BIT OF BISCUIT?**

The first pockets weren't even attached to clothes: They were small pouches that tied around the waist to hold belongings. But the pouches were easy targets for thieves, and in the 1600s clothes makers started sewing pouches directly into garments. Unfortunately, they only put them in men's pants.

By the 19th century, enormous skirts went out of style and slim silhouettes were in. That left no room for pockets, which had started being incorporated into skirts in the 17th century. Where would women put all the items they wanted to carry with them? It wasn't long before the purse was invented ... though modern women might prefer pockets to lugging a bag around.

NECKTIES

DID YOU GET THE **MEMO?**

Men around the world knot neckties as they dress each morning, but most probably have no idea why their professional attire isn't considered complete without a skinny strip of fabric circling their neck. And they're not alone. The necktie has always been something of a mystery.

TERRA-COTTA WARRIOR

In 210 B.C., China's first emperor, Qin Shi Huang Di, wanted his army to be buried with him to protect him in the afterlife. Luckily for the soldiers, the emperor settled for life-size replicas. When more than 7,000 of these terra-cotta warriors were unearthed in 1974 in Xi'an, China, many were wearing what looked like silk cloths around their necks. Were they a badge of honor? A way to keep the warriors warm? Nobody knows.

74

I'M SO FLY IT HURTS!

And in the 1630s, Croatia sent soldiers to France wearing colorful, knotted neck cloths. The French must have thought *Ooh la la!* because they ditched their starched, ruffled shirt collars in favor of the new style. These cravats became all the rage.

Early cravats looks like big lace bibs— some were six feet (1.8 m) long. In mid-18th-century England, fancy fashionistos known as macaronis wore diamond-studded high heels and cravats topped with huge bows. Historians think these men were the inspiration for the lyrics of "Yankee Doodle Dandy." Necktie fashions have evolved since then, with various widths, lengths, and knots coming and going. Today's ties are more conservative, but bold colors or patterns can still make a fashion statement.

Bet You Didn't Know

In the 18th and early 19th centuries, some men swapped their cravats for stocks, long pieces of cloth that wound around the neck, and looked a lot like the medical collars worn by people suffering neck injuries today.

TIME TO
WORK ON
THAT TAN!

Bet You Didn't Know
The most expensive
swimsuit in the
world is studded
with diamonds
worth $30 million.

SWIMSUITS

A **Revealing** History

Ever complain about how hot it is at the beach? Imagine how broiling it would be if you were wearing wool! That's what you would have worn to take a dip during the Victorian era.

Women's bathing costumes at the time were composed of a full-length dress, a corset, leggings, and special shoes. But for some extra-shy swimmers, all that coverage wasn't modest enough. They only entered the water in bathing machines, enclosed wooden carts that were rolled into the water with the swimmer inside to protect her from prying eyes.

As time passed, swimming became increasingly popular—but paddling around in heavy wool dresses didn't. In 1907, one bold beachgoer had had enough. Annette Kellerman, an Australian professional swimmer, dared to wear a form-fitting, ankle-length one-piece outfit to the beach. Police officers arrested her for public indecency, but the incident began a new trend. Women started clamoring for Kellerman's "scandalous" one-piece.

Over the next few decades, swimsuits kept shrinking. First, they were reduced to tank top and short sets. Then, fabric rationing during World War II led to the removal of the middle of women's suits. French designer Louis Réard released the first bikini in 1946. The public was outraged. But when celebrities like Brigitte Bardot were photographed wearing bikinis, women everywhere followed—*ahem*—suit. Though all kinds of styles are available today, the bikini still rules the pool.

ANNETTE KELLERMAN

HATERS GONNA **HATE.**

77

Laundry DAY

I f you dread doing the laundry, be grateful you live in modern times. Before the washing machine was invented, laundry was a backbreaking job that could take days. People had to haul heavy water, heat it on the stove, then scrub the clothes—with homemade soap, of course. After rinsing, wringing, and laying them out to dry, it's a wonder anybody thought clean clothes were worth the effort.

Washing Machine

In the Victorian era, a lot of people tried to solve the laundry problem. By 1875, more than 2,000 patents had been granted for clothes-washing devices that stomped, wrung, and raked clothes clean. All were powered by hand—except for one, in California, U.S.A., that used donkey-powered machines (it was also likely the world's first Laundromat). A reliable electric washing machine wouldn't be invented until the mid-1930s.

Clothespin

People used to lay their wet clothes over branches and hedges to dry. That often left their garments full of leaves— and the occasional critter. Sailors may actually have inspired the switch to clotheslines: They would hang their wet garments in the rigging of their ships. People improved the method by using wooden clamps to keep drying laundry from blowing away. The first spring-powered clothespin was patented in 1853.

FINALLY I GET A BREAK!

Dryer

Before the clothes dryer, people squeezed moisture out of their clothes by hand—or if they were lucky, with hand-cranked wringers. Then they'd hang their clean laundry outside and hope for good weather. Around 1800, an early clothes dryer called a ventilator allowed people to dry clothes no matter the weather. But it was a lot of work and very slow: It consisted of a barrel with holes in it that had to be hand-cranked over a fire.

Iron

In the early days, people didn't just iron to smooth out wrinkles. Hot irons killed parasites like fleas and lice, as well as bacteria and mildew growing in fabric. Ancient Romans tried pounding wrinkles out with a paddle; ancient Greeks embraced creases and used a heated round bar to create pleats on their robes. By the 14th century, Europeans were heating a piece of metal attached to a handle in the fire and using it to smooth their clothes.

CHAPTER 4

Tools

Three million years ago, on the shores of Lake Turkana in Kenya, Africa, an ancient, apelike human smashed one rock against another. Working carefully, he or she flaked off pieces of stone until one end of the rock was shaped into a point. It was humankind's first tool. And people have been dreaming up innovative, strange, and useful devices ever since.

CANDLES

Let There Be Light

It's hard to imagine life before electric lighting. When the sun went down, the light went with it. Whatever you did after that had to happen by the light of a candle.

NIGHT NIGHT!

Candles have been around since at least 3000 B.C., but they used to look very different than they do today. The first candles were called rushlights; they were made of meadow reeds cut into strips about 1.5 feet (0.5 m) long and dipped into animal fat. People put rushlights in metal holders and lit the ends.

Around the first century A.D., the Romans developed candles with wicks. The best were made of beeswax, but they were expensive. As candles spread through Europe, most people made them of tallow, the fat of animals like cattle or sheep. But tallow stank, burned with uneven light, and melted quickly. Keeping a tallow candle burning meant trimming the wick up to 40 times an hour. And a really big household, like a castle, could go through hundreds of candles a week. It was such a demanding job that nobles employed full-time "snuff servants" to keep the candles burning.

In the late 18th century, people discovered that oil from sperm whales could be turned into clean-smelling wax that gave a bright light. Sperm whales were nearly hunted to extinction before candlemakers discovered substitute ingredients, like soybean wax. Today, we no longer need candles for light, but we still enjoy their warm glow.

What's in a Name?

Since the snuff servants who cared for candles in the Middle Ages often accidentally put candles out when trimming them, "snuff" now means "extinguish."

PENS
The **Write** Stuff

NAILED IT **AGAIN**

The ancient Egyptians were remarkable innovators, dreaming up everything from hoops (see page 14) to pie (see page 50). So it's no surprise that by about 2500 B.C., they had figured out how to fill hollow reeds with ink made of soot, lamp oil, or gelatin from donkey bones and use them to scratch out hieroglyphs.

It would be thousands of years before other cultures developed the same idea. In the 13th century B.C., the Greeks were etching on clay or wax tablets with a stylus. By the first millennium B.C., the Chinese were inking elegant characters with brushes.

The Western world didn't get writing implements until the sixth century B.C., when someone figured out that nature had already come up with the perfect pen design: feathers.

A feather has a hollow center that can be dipped in ink, which then flows out as the tip moves across the page. Quill pens worked so well that they were the favored writing tool in Europe until the 19th century.

The next truly new pen didn't hit the page until the 1940s. That's when Hungarian inventor Laszlo Biro discovered that a ball bearing could roll out ink without smudging, spotting, or drying up. Makers of these ballpoint pens marketed their implements' ability to write anywhere—even at high altitudes, underwater, or upside down. By 1952, 42 million ballpoint pens were *rolling* off shelves every year.

Bet You **Didn't Know**

The Declaration of Independence was written with a quill pen.

WELCOME TO **THE FUTURE**

SPATULA

Stirrer, Scooper ... Surgical Tool?

You've probably used a spatula to flip eggs or spread frosting on a cake. So it might surprise you to learn that the first spatulas were medical devices, not kitchen tools.

Early spatulas were made out of bronze, with a point at one end and a broad flat blade at the other end. Around the first century A.D., ancient pharmacists used the pointed side to mix up medicines and then the blade to apply the concoction to the aching body part.

Physicians quickly discovered that the tool had all kinds of uses. They used spatulas as tongue depressors to peer down swollen throats, or heated them in a flame and held them against wounds to cauterize, or burn, them. This practice stopped bleeding and prevented infection, but in the days before anesthesia, it must have been agonizing. Spatulas were so commonly used that every surviving ancient text on medical writing from Greece and Rome mentions them at least once.

It didn't take long for cooks to realize that spatulas were also perfect for all kinds of kitchen tasks, from flipping fish to mixing batter. They became so popular that they were nicknamed "child cheaters" for their ability to scrape all traces of batter out of a bowl, leaving none for little fingers to scoop up.

I'M **GOING IN!**

Bet You **Didn't Know**

When archaeologists peered inside the skull of a 2,600-year-old mummy using a CT scanner, they were shocked to find a spatula his embalmers had left behind.

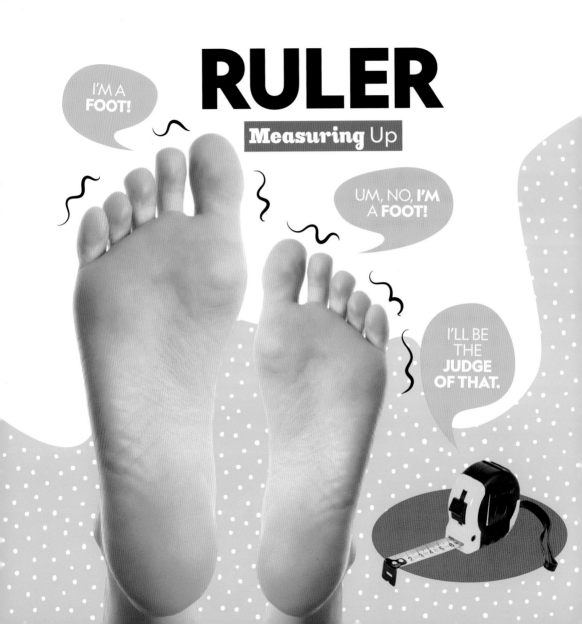

Before there were rulers or measuring tapes, how did people know the length of anything? In ancient times, different parts of the human body were used for measuring. One of the earliest measurements was the cubit, defined as the distance from a man's elbow to the top of his middle finger. A mile was said to be the length of a thousand paces. And a foot was, well, the length of a human foot.

The only problem was that people have different-sized arms, feet, and paces. When building projects started getting ambitious—like the massive cathedrals of the Middle Ages—a standard system of measurement became necessary.

In the 13th century, England's King Edward I created a master yardstick made of iron, called the Iron Ulna. Medieval English towns kept replicas of the stick attached to their town halls or gates, and builders used them to create their own yardsticks. By decree, anyone unable to travel into town could use three ears of corn laid end to end as a substitute measurement.

Standardized measurement across the world didn't become a reality until 1791. That's when the French Academy of Sciences created the standardized meter: a length one ten-millionth the distance from the Equator to the North Pole on a line crossing through Paris. In 1983, the academy updated the measurement to the distance that light travels in 1/299,792,458 of a second.

KING HENRY I

THAT'S WHAT I CALL A **RULE OF THUMB!**

What's in **a Name?**

King Henry I is said to have decreed that a yard was the distance from the tip of his nose to his outstretched thumb.

WHAT'S IN YOUR Tool Box?

Can you imagine trying to chop wood or nail two boards together without an ax, a saw, or a hammer? Of course not! Many of the implements we take for granted today were millions of years in the making.

Ax

By about 30,000 B.C., our ancestors were attaching wooden handles to sharpened stones to create the first axes. Over time, they figured out how to form and shape metal into stronger blades, which made the iron axes of the Middle Ages possible. Those improved axes allowed people to clear huge areas of forest, beginning the age of modern farming.

Hammer

Have you ever used a rock as a makeshift hammer? If so, you were hammering the same way early humans did for thousands of years. Archaeologists have discovered stone hammers dating back 3.3 million years on the shores of Kenya's Lake Turkana in Africa. Early humans also used these hammers to chip flakes off other rocks, forming more sophisticated tools like blades for cutting.

IT'S HAMMER TIME!

NOW THAT'S WHAT I CALL A **CUTTING-EDGE** DISCOVERY!

ARCHIMEDES' SCREW

Saw

According to an ancient Greek myth, the first saw was made by a boy named Perdix, who was inspired to create the tool after observing the ridges on a fish's backbone. In reality, people were using saws 2,000 years before that: The ancient Egyptians had copper saw blades that could cut wood and even stone. The saw's basic design hasn't changed in thousands of years.

Screw

The first screw didn't attach two objects together; it was invented for moving water. Created by the ancient Greek scientist Archimedes, the screw could remove water from the hold of a ship. It consisted of a large corkscrew inside a circular pipe. When a person turned a handle, the corkscrew would spin, pulling water up and out of the ship.

TELESCOPE

Eye to **the Sky**

Bet You **Didn't Know**

The first images the Hubble telescope beamed back to Earth were blurry, due to a fault in one of its lenses. Astronauts performed a space walk to fit Hubble with a pair of "space glasses," and the telescope has had perfect vision ever since.

I SPY WITH MY LITTLE EYE …

Before 17th-century Italian scientist Galileo Galilei came along, there was no good way to get a look at faraway objects. Sailors could squint into a type of early telescope called a spyglass, which was a tube with a piece of curved glass at one end. But since it only magnified objects to three times their size, it wasn't much help in spotting land—or glimpsing marauding pirate ships before it was too late.

Galileo thought he could do better. In 1609, he experimented with looking through multiple lenses together and came up with a design that magnified objects to 30 times their size. Galileo used his invention to observe the sky, becoming the first person to use a telescope to study astronomy.

WON'T SAY I TOLD YOU SO, **BUT** …

GALILEO GALILEI

He observed that the planet Venus goes through different phases—something that wouldn't be possible if Earth was at the center of the universe, as most people at the time—especially leaders of the powerful Catholic Church—believed. Galileo had found proof that the sun is at the center of the universe and all the planets orbit around it. That got him in big trouble with the church. Under threat of torture, Galileo conceded and said he'd been mistaken: Earth didn't move around the sun after all. But as the Renaissance rebel left the courtroom, witnesses heard him mutter, "All the same, it moves."

It took the Catholic Church 359 years to admit that Galileo had been right. In the meantime, astronomers made bigger and better telescopes that could see even deeper into space. But they were limited by Earth's atmosphere, which distorts images. Astronomers dreamed of a telescope that could float in space and see into the farthest corners of the universe. In 1990, NASA launched the Hubble Space Telescope, which has since discovered distant galaxies, exploding stars, and even the birthday of the universe: 13.8 billion years ago.

CELL PHONE

Signals Through Space

On April 3, 1973, Motorola Corporation engineer Martin Cooper made the first ever mobile phone call. The device he spoke into was more than 14 inches (35.5 cm) from its base to the tip of its antenna, and it weighed almost 2.5 pounds (1.1 kg). Carrying it around all day would have been an arm workout!

Cell phone technology got its start more than 100 years before that first call. In 1843, chemist Michael Faraday had the idea that air could conduct electricity. People thought he was crazy. But 22 years later, a scientist named Mahlon Loomis proved Faraday right when he sent the first ever wireless message zipping through the atmosphere, using two kites flying on mountains 18 miles (29 km) apart.

1980s, YOU THERE?

MESSAGE RECEIVED!

Mobile phone technology began in earnest in the 1980s. Early models cost thousands of dollars. They became a status symbol for Wall Street stockbrokers, who flashed their wealth by screaming into their bulky, bricklike handheld phones.

In 2007, Apple Inc. introduced the iPhone. For the first time, a phone, computer, and multimedia device were combined—and the way people used their cell phones changed forever. Today, Americans check their phones a total of eight billion times a day. And between the videos, apps, and music, it's easy to forget they make calls, too.

Bet You **Didn't Know**

Nearly all mobile phones in Japan are waterproof—so people can use them in the shower!

95

CAMERA

Snap Happy

Bet You Didn't Know

Today, satellites can take sneaky photos from above. During World Wars I and II, that job went to carrier pigeons that flew with tiny cameras strapped to their bodies.

SOME ASSEMBLY REQUIRED

Modern cameras are sophisticated pieces of technology. But the first cameras were something you can make yourself with a cardboard box.

Called a camera obscura, Latin for "dark chamber," the device let light into a box through a small hole, and projected an inverted image from outside onto a screen. The first people to use camera obscuras were Arab astronomers who wanted to observe the sun without damaging their eyes by looking at it directly. Also known as pinhole cameras, they're still a popular way of viewing a solar eclipse today.

By the 18th century, many artists were using camera obscuras to project images onto paper. Then they would simply trace the outlines on the page. Some art experts think 17th-century Dutch painter Johannes (Jan) Vermeer used a camera obscura to create his ultrarealistic paintings—unlike other artists of his era, Vermeer's paintings portray distance with startling accuracy.

Around the same time artists were using camera obscuras, scientists discovered that certain chemicals change when exposed to light. In 1826, French chemist Joseph Niépce coated a plate with a light-sensitive substance called bitumen of Judea and inserted it in his camera obscura. Niépce let his photo expose for eight hours. The bitumen that was hit with light hardened. When he washed away the unhardened bitumen, he was left with a grainy image of the view out his attic window in Burgundy. It's the world's oldest existing photograph.

These days, we can snap a series of selfies in seconds, but for the earliest photographs, long exposure times made posing a marathon event. Subjects had to sit perfectly still for as long as 15 minutes. Sometimes photographers even used a clamp to hold peoples' heads steady.

SAY CHEESE! FOR A REALLY LONG TIME ...

VELCRO

From **Irritation** to **Invention**

When Swiss mountaineer George de Mestral returned from a hike with his dog one summer day in 1948, he noticed that his canine companion had picked up some unwanted hitchhikers on the way: Clinging burrs were stuck all over its fur. Most people might have picked them off and tossed them away in annoyance. But not de Mestral.

De Mestral took the burrs and peered at them under a microscope. He saw that each one was covered with thousands of tiny hooks that allowed the burr to firmly attach itself to almost anything. Then de Mestral had an aha moment! He realized that if he could create a product that did the same thing, he would have a fastener to rival the zipper.

Actually creating a synthetic burr imitation wasn't easy. It took de Mestral nearly 10 years of research and experiments

I AM TRULY AN INSPIRATION.

98

until he finally hit on the perfect design: Two strips of fabric, one with thousands of tiny hooks and another with thousands of tiny loops. He called it Velcro, after the French words *velours*, meaning "velvet," and *crochet*, meaning "hook."

Velcro took off—literally—in the early 1960s, when NASA saw its potential uses in outer space. It was used in spacecraft to hold pens, food packets, and anything else astronauts didn't want floating around in zero gravity. Velcro has stuck with us ever since.

Bet You **Didn't Know**

The U.S. Army uses a nearly silent version of Velcro on soldiers' uniforms.

99

WINDSHIELD
WIPERS

Clearing the Way

Bet You **Didn't Know**

Windshield wiper inventor Mary Anderson finally got credit for her creation in 2011, when she was inducted into the Inventors Hall of Fame.

MARY ANDERSON

I'M COMING FOR YOU, **RAIN.**

In the winter of 1902, a woman named Mary Anderson took her first trip to New York City. After traveling all the way from Birmingham, Alabama, U.S.A., she boarded a trolley car to take in the marvels of skyscrapers and streets bustling with crowds.

But Anderson's view was ... disappointing. Snow was blowing against the trolley car's windows, ruining her sightseeing. Anderson noticed that it was creating problems for the car's driver, too. He had to keep stopping to wipe down the windshield by hand.

Back then, trolley windshields were divided into multiple panes. If one of them got obstructed by rain or snow, the driver could open it to clear his line of sight—but that let in the weather, drenching the driver and passengers sitting near the front. The window system worked so poorly that in really bad weather, drivers like Anderson's had to take matters into their own hands.

Right there in her seat on the trolley car, Anderson started to sketch out an idea: a rubber blade that would drag across the windshield when the driver pulled a lever near his steering wheel. At the time, her device didn't catch on. In fact, companies told Anderson that her invention would just distract drivers. But history proved her right soon enough: By 1916, windshield wipers were standard on most vehicles.

YOU'RE MY **HERO,** MARY!

ACCIDENTAL Inventions

Some inventors tinker for decades until they come up with something that works. Others stumble on great ideas by accident. Read on to see how a few blunders became some of history's greatest best sellers.

NOW THAT'S A **BONE-A FIDE** IDEA!

1895 X-Ray Images

German physicist Wilhelm Röntgen was experimenting with gas-filled glass tubes called cathode ray tubes in 1895. When he ran electricity through the gas, the tubes would glow ... and so would a piece of fluorescent cardboard across the room. Röntgen realized that the cathode ray tubes were shooting out invisible rays (he termed them "x-rays" because *x* in math refers to an unknown) that could pass through paper, wood, and—most significantly—skin, revealing the bones beneath.

1880 1890 1900 1910 1920

PENICILLIN
100 mg
PENICILLIN

A scientist named Alexander Fleming was growing bacteria on plates so he could study them when he made a mistake: He left one of the plates uncovered and went on vacation. When Fleming returned, he noticed that mold had taken over the plate—and somehow, it had stopped the bacteria from growing. His error turned out to be the accidental discovery of the world's first antibiotic: penicillin. Since then, the drug has saved an estimated 200 million lives.

1920 Penicillin

Ruth Wakefield, co-owner of the Toll House Inn in Whitman, Massachusetts, U.S.A., was baking chocolate cookies for her guests one day when—*uh-oh*—she ran out of powdered baker's chocolate. So she grabbed the closest thing she had: a bar of semisweet chocolate. She broke the bar up into chunks, stirred them into the batter, and crossed her fingers. When the timer dinged, Wakefield pulled out the world's first chocolate chip cookies. Her recipe still appears on the back of bags of Nestlé chocolate chips.

1938
Chocolate Chip Cookies

1956
Play-Doh

Colorful, moldable Play-Doh didn't start out for kids. A company named Kutol Products invented it to remove soot stains left by coal stoves on wallpaper. That changed when the company discovered that children were playing with it. Kutol switched gears, added fun colors, and created one of the most beloved toys of all time.

| 1930 | 1940 | 1950 | 1960 | 1970 |

1951
Super Glue

Harry Coover, a researcher for the Eastman Kodak Company, was in a sticky situation in 1942. He was trying to come up with a material to create clear gunsights for U.S. soldiers in World War II. But the substance he was experimenting with, cyanoacrylate, wasn't working: It just stuck to everything. Frustrated, Coover abandoned the idea—until he encountered the substance in experiments again in 1951, and he finally realized he had the perfect glue on his hands. Super Glue hit shelves in 1958.

CHAPTER 5

Symbols & Manners

Achoo! "Gesundheit!"

"I give you this ring as a sign of my love."

"How do you do?"

You might not realize it, but age-old customs and symbols are a fundamental part of our lives, from special events to every day moments. Whether you're introducing yourself with a firm handshake, trying out a new hair place, or reacting to someone's sneeze, you're carrying on time-honored traditions. Want to know what they are?

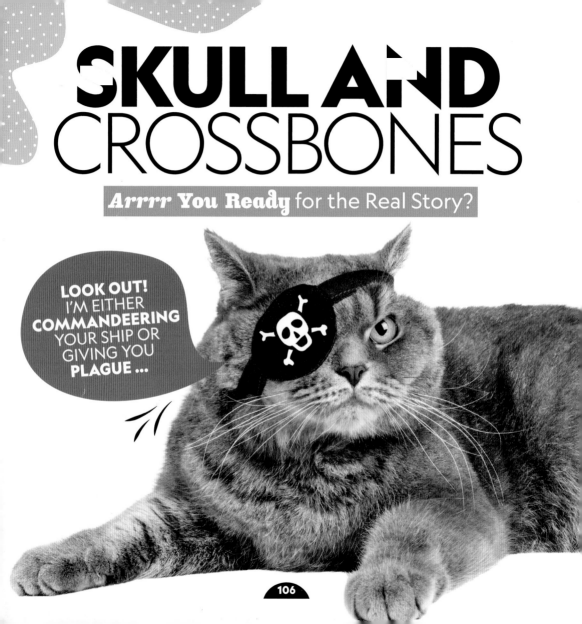

When a label features a skull atop two crossed bones, it's a warning that there's something deadly inside. And the same symbol brings to mind black flags and peg-legged pirates sailing the seven seas. What's the connection?

In October 1347, people gathered on the docks of Messina, Italy, to greet 12 arriving trading ships. But the warm welcome turned to horror when they discovered most of the sailors were dead, and the survivors were delirious with pain and fever. They were also covered in strange black boils that gave the illness its nick-name: the Black Death. Over the next five years, the disease killed more than 20 million Europeans—about one in every three people. Since death was everywhere, skull-and-crossbones art and decor became common.

The symbol spread from land to sea, as captains used it in their ship's logs to note which sailors died on board.

Bet You Didn't Know

Not all pirates used the skull and crossbones. Some decorated their flags with other spooky symbols like skeletons, spears, and bleeding hearts.

In the 18th century, pirates began hoisting black flags called Jolly Rogers painted with the skull and crossbones. The symbol of death was meant to frighten sailors. It worked.

In 1829, a law passed in New York State, U.S.A., required that all poisonous substances had to be labeled. Manufacturers started using the skull and crossbones around 1850. If you see one today, watch out—you're either handling something toxic or a band of buccaneers is about to invade.

APPLAUSE

Sounding Off

Put your hands together for this international symbol of approval. How long have people been clapping? Nobody knows. But historians do know that applause has been around for a long, long time.

In ancient Rome, politicians became skilled at gauging their popularity based on the volume and enthusiasm of applause from the crowd. It was the ancestor of today's political polls. And Roman citizens didn't limit themselves to just hitting their hands together. They also cheered by snapping their fingers, flapping the edges of their togas, and humming so that a group sounded like a swarm of bees.

Bet You Didn't Know

Humans aren't the only primates that put their hands together. Gorillas, chimpanzees, and other great apes sometimes clap to draw attention.

WHAT'S ALL THE BUZZ ABOUT?

Rome's theatrical plays ended with the chief actor yelling *"Valete et plaudite!"* (Latin for "Goodbye and applause!") to encourage the audience to show praise for the show. To make themselves look more successful, actors sometimes hired professional clappers to infiltrate the audience and encourage those around them to applaud longer and louder. They even used hired hands to boo and hiss at their enemies' performances.

WE DONE YET? MY HANDS ARE STARTING TO **HURT!**

By the 19th century, theaters were crammed with people paid to laugh at jokes, sob during sad scenes, and call for encores at the end. Of course, this fake appreciation still exists today—laugh tracks are sometimes added to TV shows or online videos to help viewers get giggling.

BARBER
POLE

A **Gory** Story

COME TAKE **A SEAT** ...

Today, the sight of a spinning red-white-and-blue pole tells you a barbershop is nearby. But in medieval times, the same icon might have made you tremble in fear: It often meant you were in for more than just a trim.

Back then, barbers didn't just cut hair—they also pulled teeth, performed surgery, and amputated limbs. But their most popular procedure was bloodletting. At the time, people believed that having too much blood in the body could cause ailments like fevers or plague. They thought getting rid of some of that pesky blood would make them healthy.

Barbers would have patients grip a pole, making their veins stand out for easy cutting. When enough blood had been drained, they would stop the flow with white cloths.

After the patient wobbled weakly away, the barber would hang the stained red cloths to dry from the pole outside. Blowing breezes would make the cloths wrap around the pole, and those colorful spirals have symbolized barbershops ever since.

Eventually, people figured out that bloodletting was a bad idea. Barbers gave up cutting into their patients' blue veins to focus on hair, but the symbol of their old work stuck. Many barbers today still advertise their craft—and its gruesome past— with a spinning red-white-and-blue sign.

GOT **A LICENSE** FOR THAT POLE?

Bet You **Didn't Know**

In some U.S. states, it's illegal to display a barber pole outside a business unless a licensed barber works inside.

SALUTE

Atten-**tion!**

Members of the U.S. military have a lot to remember when it's time to show respect with a salute. The right hand must snap to the forehead at a 45-degree angle, palm down. Sailors on ships only salute at the first meeting of the day. Ranking officers don't return salutes. So what's the story behind the gesture?

Experts think the salute likely dates back to the Roman Empire, when high-profile assassinations were common. Emperor Julius Caesar famously went from beloved to expired in just five years! Understandably, Roman leaders were a little jumpy. It became customary for a citizen approaching an officer to raise his hand to show he wasn't holding a weapon.

Over time, the gesture evolved. It became tradition in the British Army for lower-ranking soldiers to remove their hats to greet officers. But it wasn't always practical for soldiers to stop what they were doing and salute, so in 1745, the rules relaxed and soldiers were permitted to simply touch their caps and bow.

HANDS WHERE I CAN **SEE 'EM!**

The British Army and Royal Air Force saluted with the palm facing outward, but the Royal Navy did things a little differently. Back then, working on a ship involved sealing the ship's hull with tar and pitch—messy work. So sailors saluted with their palms down to avoid showing stained hands. The U.S. military took a shine to this style in the early 1800s, and it's been the official symbol of respect ever since.

POLICE OFFICER

Bet You **Didn't Know**

Soldiers are excused from saluting if their hands are full.

HANDSHAKE

A **Gripping** History

When you meet a new person, extending your arm for a handshake is almost automatic. But if you think about it, we could also rub our foreheads together or stand back-to-back and wiggle. Why do we grasp each other's hands and move them up and down?

One theory is that, like dogs exchanging greetings, we shake hands to get a whiff of the other person's scent. A 2015 study found that after shaking hands with someone, people often unconsciously bring their hands to their faces. When people were fitted with nasal devices to measure airflow, the researchers figured out what they were doing: sniffing their hands!

Scientists think that we might sneakily sniff a new acquaintance in order to gather chemical signals carried in their scent.

Handshakes have been around for thousands of years, and they probably got their start as a way for people to say "I come in peace." By extending an empty right hand, the greeter showed that he wasn't holding a weapon. Some people even think that the pumping, up-and-down motion was originally intended to dislodge any knives hidden in a sleeve.

Bet You **Didn't Know**

George Washington thought handshakes were unrefined and chose to bow instead.

UMM, **HARD PASS**

GEORGE WASHINGTON

Today, people all around the world shake hands—but not in exactly the same way. In Japan, you might be greeted with a bow along with a handshake. In India, people use two hands to grasp another person's in greeting. And the French often forgo handshakes entirely for a double-cheek kiss.

BODY LANGUAGE Decoded

Has anyone ever teased you for talking with your hands? Or waving your arms dramatically? Words aren't the only way we communicate. While dogs may wag their tails or twitch their ears to get a point across, people make all kinds of gestures.

Thumbs-Up

You probably think nothing of making a thumbs-up to show appreciation. But in the fourth century B.C., the gesture meant life or death. At gladiator battles, spectators put their thumbs up if they thought a warrior had fought bravely and deserved to live. A thumbs-down, on the other hand, meant the defeated warrior would be executed.

High Five

The first version of a high five was actually the low five. Called slapping skin, it was popular among musicians in the jazz age of the 1920s. Multiple people claim credit for the first true high five: One story says it started with the Los Angeles Dodgers baseball team; another says basketball players in Louisville, Kentucky, U.S.A., first smacked their palms together during the 1978–79 season.

¯_(ツ)_/¯

Shrugging the Shoulders

Lifting shoulders while raising palms skyward is one of the most universal human gestures. Scientists think that it's also one of the oldest—it's been passed down through our lineage for hundreds of millions of years: Ancient reptiles would push their spines downward to show submission. Today, chimpanzees use it to indicate helplessness and ask for food.

Crossing Your Fingers

I'M FEELING LUCKY!

The symbol of the cross has been powerful since long before Christianity. Early Europeans thought that if they made a wish in front of a cross, it would come true. When a cross wasn't available, people used their hands to mimic the cross and make their own symbol of luck. Sometimes two people would create a single cross by placing their index fingers together at right angles. Over time, it evolved into a solo gesture.

GESUNDHEIT!

Sneeze Secrets

When you hear the sound *achoo!* it's almost always followed by a *"Gesundheit"* or "Bless you." That's because most of us have been taught not responding to a sneeze would be rude. But we don't answer other bodily noises, such as burps. So what makes a sneeze special?

ACHOO!

The word "gesund-heit" is German for "healthiness." Germany is just one of many cultures that wishes good health when someone sneezes. The ancient Greeks told each other "long life." Hindus say "live well." The Chinese say *Bai sui,* meaning "May you live 100 years." And in many Spanish-speaking cultures, one sneeze earns you a *salud* (health), a double sneeze gets *dinero* (wealth), and a third *amor* (love).

People began wishing each other good health because in many ancient cultures it was believed that a sneeze could blow a person's soul straight out of their body. Uttering the right phrase was like a magical spell that protected evil spirits from stealing the sneezer's soul.

BEGONE, PLAGUE!

POPE CLEMENT VI

The phrase "God bless you" in response to a sneeze came from Rome during the plague of A.D. 590. Even though people didn't yet know that sneezes can spread disease-causing microbes, they did recognize that when a person started sniffling, he or she often came down with the plague shortly after. People began saying "God bless you" as a quick prayer to protect the person from getting sick, and the idea stuck. Pope Clement VI is known to have said it to sufferers of the Black Death of 1348–49. So the next time someone offers a polite response to your sneeze, they're really wishing you good health—and hoping that you don't have the plague!

Bet You **Didn't Know**

A single sneeze can produce up to 40,000 saliva droplets.

WEDDING RINGS

Circles of **Love**

Most ancient Egyptian traditions are no longer practiced. People don't typically build pyramids or mummify the dead. But one ancient Egyptian ritual is still going strong today: the exchange of rings during a wedding ceremony.

A circle, because it has no beginning or end, has long been a symbol of eternal love. Historians think that about 6,000 years ago, love-struck Egyptians plucked grasses and reeds from alongside the Nile River and twisted them into rings. The hole in the ring's center was a representation of a gateway leading to the future. While love may last forever, these grass rings did not. People switched to more durable materials like leather, bone, or ivory. Some believed the more valuable the ring, the stronger the love.

The Egyptians and Romans believed that a vein called the *vena amoris* ran directly from the fourth finger of the left hand to the heart, so that's where they wore their rings. Though today we know that no such vein exists, many people still wear their wedding band on that finger.

Bet You **Didn't Know**

Not all cultures put wedding rings on the fourth finger of the left hand. Married Hindu women wear toe rings to signify their status.

In ancient Rome, wedding rings weren't exactly a token of love: They symbolized a husband's legal ownership of his wife. Roman wives wore gold rings at social events, but they swapped the fancy jewelry for sturdier iron versions at home. Men didn't start wearing wedding rings until World War II, when many newly married soldiers sported them as a reminder of their wives back home. By the mid-20th century, wedding rings for both men and women were quite common.

BE MINE ...

BIRTHDAY
CAKE

Treat Yourself

O n your last birthday, chances are you blew out some candles and then enjoyed a slice—or maybe a few!—of delicious cake. But did you ever stop to wonder where this sweet tradition came from?

MORE **CHEESE** ON YOUR CAKE?

Ancient Egyptians didn't invent the cake—but they did come up with the idea of birthdays. When a new pharaoh was crowned, Egyptians believed that he or she was born again as a god. This "birth" day was a cause for celebration. The ancient Greeks were the first to realize that you can't have a proper party without cake. To honor the moon goddess Artemis, they decorated cakes with candles to mimic moonlight.

OMG, THANKS, **DEVOTEES!**

STATUE OF ARTEMIS

It was the ancient Romans who put the two traditions together. But a Roman birthday cake tasted a little different from today's: A surviving recipe for a 50th birthday cake lists wheat flour, olive oil, honey, and grated cheese as ingredients.

The first modern birthday cakes appeared in Germany, where families marked the anniversary of their children's births with a celebration called *kinderfest*. In the morning, the birthday boy or girl would be presented with a cake already lit with candles—one for each year of their life, plus one to grow on. After letting the candles burn all day, it was finally time to make a wish, blow them out, and dig in. Happy birthday!

DAYLIGHT SAVING TIME

I DID IT FOR **THE LULZ!**

Most traditions continue because people like them. After all, who would say no to lighting firecrackers to celebrate the Chinese New Year or hunting for eggs left behind by a big bunny? But there's one tradition that's still going strong even though not everyone approves of it. It's daylight saving time.

When daylight saving time begins in the spring, it adds an extra hour of glorious sunlight to warm nights. But when it comes time to set the clocks back an hour in the autumn, many people dread the darkness that falls by late afternoon. If you're one of them, you can blame Benjamin Franklin.

In 1784, Franklin was an American envoy in Paris, France, 78 years old, and ... a little grumpy. Though famous for being a champion of "early to bed and early to rise," the Founding Father didn't exactly follow his own advice. So when the summer sun annoyingly woke him at 6 a.m., he took up his pen to write a wisecracking essay. Franklin explained to Parisians that if they started the day at dawn and went to bed earlier, they could save the modern-day equivalent of $200 million in candles. He even suggested that cannons should be fired every morning to make sure even the laziest people were up and at 'em.

Franklin's essay was sarcastic, but 130 years later, when World War I struck, the energy-saving idea made sense. On April 30, 1916, Germany enacted daylight saving time to conserve electricity during wartime. The United States followed a few years later. And people have been forgetting to change their clocks ever since.

WE'RE GOOD, **THANKS.**

Bet You Didn't Know

Hawaii and Arizona don't observe daylight saving time.

Table Manners

THROUGH TIME

Do your parents constantly remind you not to put your elbows on the table, to put your napkin in your lap, and to wait until everyone is served before picking up your fork? Check out some of this heinous etiquette throughout history. Next time you get nagged about your manners, you can point out it could be a whole lot worse.

300
Dogs at Dinner

Think it's rude when a pet pooch begs for scraps at the table? In ancient Greece, it was standard practice. Vases from the time show that people brought their animals to dinner with them. Napkins hadn't been invented yet, so when diners had finished eating, they would wipe their hands on scraps of bread, then throw it to the waiting pets.

A.D. 1   200   400   600   800

A.D. 50
Taste Test

You might think it's rude for someone to take a bite of your food before you've even tried it. But leaders have been employing official taste testers to make sure their meals are safe to eat for centuries. History's most famous food taster was Halotus, who worked for the Roman emperor Claudius. He failed at his job in A.D. 54 when Claudius died of poisoning— but some think Halotus was part of the plot.

IT'S A PRETTY **SWEET GIG.**

126

YOU **DO NOT** WANNA LOOK IN HERE ...

Nowadays, if you need to use the bathroom during a meal, you excuse yourself and leave the table. But centuries ago in England, you wouldn't have to miss a minute of the party. It was fashionable at the time for lavish meals to continue for up to five hours. There was no indoor plumbing, but hosts made sure to provide plenty of chamber pots. In the dining room. How thoughtful.

MODERN DAY
No More Double Dipping

Once your chip or carrot has taken a dunk in the dip bowl and you've had a bite, do you consider another pass through the bowl off-limits? You should. In 2008, scientists had volunteers double dip crackers into test dips and then measured the germs that were transferred from their mouths to the bowl. Brace yourself: They found that after multiple dunks, about 10,000 bacteria were swimming in the dip. Gross!

1700s
Excuse You!

| 1000 | 1200 | 1600 | 1800 | MODERN DAY |

1300s
Who Dealt It?

Table etiquette wasn't too strict in the European Middle Ages. It was considered the height of elegance if you didn't let food spill out of your mouth, dip your fingers into the sauce, or let your hands get too greasy when tearing meat off the bone. One scholar of the day, Erasmus of Rotterdam, implored diners that, if they had to pass gas, "If it is possible to withdraw, it should be done alone. But if not ... let a cough hide the sound." Don't get any ideas!

PEE-EW!

127

CHAPTER 6

Around the House

When you get home at the end of the day, you might flip on the lights, head to the fridge for a snack, and then settle down in front of the TV. But for most of history, you couldn't have done any of that. Life at home was dark, dirty, and a lot of work. That started changing as household inventions—each with its own strange story—began to appear.

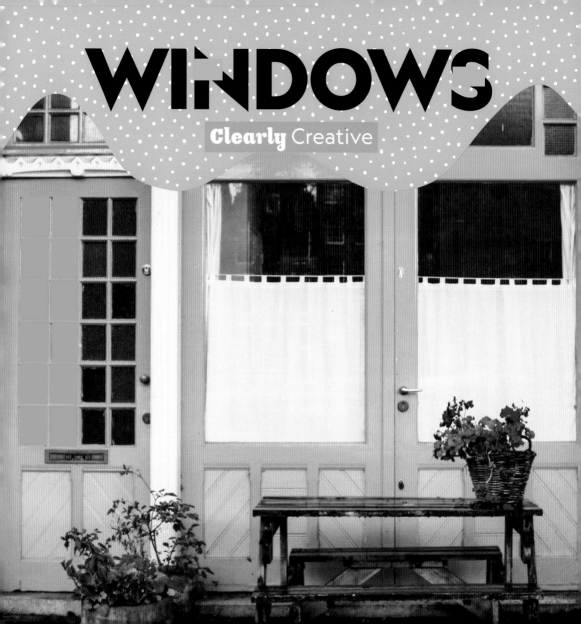

WINDOWS

Clearly Creative

Nowadays, a house without windows would be a strange sight. But just two centuries ago, the glass to make them was a rare luxury only the wealthiest could afford.

We don't know who first discovered glass, but it's possible they had just been through a hair-raising experience: Glass is sometimes created in nature by certain disasters. Volcanoes, lightning strikes, and meteorites can all cause rocks to melt and fuse into glass.

The Romans were the first people to figure out how to turn glass into window-panes: By the third century A.D., they were blowing cylinder-shaped bubbles of it, then slicing them from top to bottom and flattening them. But when the Western Roman Empire shattered in the fourth century, its glass windows went with it. The so-called Dark Ages that followed really were dark: Most people used wooden shutters to keep the cold—and the light—out.

It took a thousand years before European glassmakers rediscovered how to make flat window glass. But it was considered an extravagance: In England, people had to pay taxes on each glass window. The glass windows were so prized that when the upper classes closed their estates for the season, they had their windowpanes removed and stored until they returned. The tax was abolished in the 19th century, just in time for the most extravagant glass structure the world had yet seen: London's Crystal Palace, which amazed visitors with its 293,655 sparkling panes.

HMM, SEEMS LIKE A **STRETCH.**

Bet You **Didn't Know**

In the Middle Ages, some people soaked animal skins in oil until they were slightly see-through, then nailed them across their windows.

INDOOR
LIGHTING

A **Brilliant** Invention

IS IT ME OR IS IT **HOT IN HERE?**

For most of human history, a candlelit dinner wasn't romantic. It was necessary. If you wanted to see your dining companions—or what you were eating—you had to use some form of fire.

But open flames are incredibly dangerous. People were constantly lighting their straw mattresses, houses, and wigs on fire. By the 1870s, fires caused by indoor flames were killing up to 6,000 people a year in the United States. A safer solution was needed: electric lighting.

But electric lights are useless without something to plug them into. Edison's greatest contribution to electric lighting was developing the power grid that got lightbulbs glowing. He spent nearly a year installing a power plant and laying 15 miles (24 km) of cable in New York City. At first, horses in the area acted jumpy because faulty wiring allowed electricity to leak out of the grid and made their metal horseshoes tingle. But Edison worked out the kinks, and in 1882, he flipped the switch to light up 85 Manhattan businesses for the first time. The age of electricity had begun.

WARREN DE LA RUE

Thomas Edison usually gets the credit for creating the lightbulb. But in reality, many different inventors were working on the lightbulb at the same time. In 1840, seven years before Edison was even born, a British chemist named Warren De la Rue created one of the world's first lightbulbs when he passed an electrical current through a thin thread-like piece of platinum, called a filament, to make it glow. Platinum was too expensive to make a practical filament, so Edison raced to be the first to find an affordable material that burned brightly. After testing more than 6,000 possibilities, he lit upon the perfect thing, carbonized bamboo, in 1879.

WHAT IN TARNATION?!

Bet You Didn't Know

Thomas Edison tried just about everything during his search for a lightbulb filament—including hair from the red beard of a family friend.

133

REFRIGERATORS

A WORLD WITHOUT ME? PERISH THE THOUGHT!

Do you love a tall, cold glass of milk? Or a big bowl of chocolate ice cream? Sure, who doesn't? Now imagine what life was like before the invention of refrigeration—when none of those things was possible.

Ancient people had to get clever when it came to preserving food. Some cultures pickled, salted, smoked, or dried their dishes to discourage bacteria from growing. Others chilled their meals: As early as 1000 B.C., the ancient Chinese were cutting ice blocks and using them to keep their leftovers cold.

In the 18th century, Europeans would gather ice in the winter, salt it to help keep it frozen, and stash it underground. The method worked surprisingly well and allowed ice to stay solid for months. By Victorian times, most people had an icebox in their homes. This metal-lined container had one compartment for ice and another for food. A layer of cork, sawdust, or seaweed helped keep the chill in. Workers known as icemen would deliver replacement blocks when the ice had melted.

Refrigeration machines, invented in the 1800s, allowed ships to safely carry perishables like meat across oceans for the first time. In 1874, one was even used to cool the world's first artificial ice rink. But it took over a century for the technology to become affordable enough for home use. By the 1920s, a refrigerator was chilling in nearly every American household.

Bet You **Didn't Know**

Ancient Egyptians and Native Americans both put clay pots filled with water outside during cold nights to freeze into ancient ice packs.

SWIMMING
POOLS

Plunge Into the Past

Bet You **Didn't Know**

Guests at the Golden Nugget hotel in Las Vegas, Nevada, U.S.A., can swim in a pool wrapped around a giant shark tank—and even zip down a three-story slide that runs right through the middle of the tank!

When you take a refreshing dip in a swimming pool, you're not just cooling off. You're taking part in a tradition that dates back nearly to the beginning of civilization. People have been seeking out spots for a refreshing plunge since ancient times.

The great-great-great-grandparent of your neighborhood pool is the Great Bath of Mohenjo Daro, built in modern-day Pakistan more than 5,000 years ago. This rectangular pool was made from bricks, covered in plaster, and sealed with tar. Scholars believe it was a holy place where people would come to purify their bodies before religious rituals.

Taking a dip was part of daily life for ancient Romans. They used pools for bathing, socializing, and even for training soldiers to fight battles in water. But back then, the Latin word for "pool," *piscina*, didn't mean a place for swimming: It referred to a fishpond. And Roman children would not have jumped into the piscina to cool off because ferocious moray

eels were often kept in the water. Many Romans raised eels for eating—though some, like first-century B.C. aristocrat Vedius Pollio, also used their eel ponds as a place to toss enemies to a terrible death.

Swimming pools didn't become popular until centuries later. In 1837, six indoor pools were installed in London, England. And after the first modern Olympic Games in 1896, which included swimming races, people suddenly couldn't get enough dunking and diving. In the United States, cities constructed public pools in hopes of stopping young people from stripping naked and plunging into the local rivers and lakes. Before many homes had indoor plumbing, many people considered public pools a place to get clean. The United States' first public pool, which opened in Boston, Massachusetts, in 1869, was even called the Cabot Street Bath.

MORAY EEL

COME ON IN, KIDS, **THE WATER'S FINE!**

TELEVISION

The Big **Picture**

Television is a big part of home entertainment—the average American watches about five hours of television a day. And it took a couple of mad scientists to figure out how to make the whole thing work.

Scottish scientist John Logie Baird invented the first working television system. Baird had a lot of wild ideas: He sold shoe polish and razor blades to fund his experiments and once blew up an electrical grid while trying to make artificial diamonds. Baird came up with a "Televisor" that worked a little like a radio, but it also included a rotating mechanism that could capture video. He wired the whole thing together with scrap metal from cookie tins, knitting needles, and piano wire. In 1926, Baird held the first public demonstration of TV in London, broadcasting the face of a woman from one room to another. A journalist on the scene wondered if the system had any practical use.

WHERE'S THE **HD OPTION?**

THE FIRST TV

The first successful early TV system was the brainchild of a 21-year-old inventor named Philo Taylor Farnsworth. Born to a farming family in 1906, Farnsworth spent his childhood in a log cabin without electricity, but he quickly made up for lost time: At age 14, while plowing a potato field in straight, parallel lines, Farnsworth had the idea for a television system that would break an image into horizontal lines and reassemble it into a picture at the other end. The same basic principle still powers TVs today.

SO MANY ADS, **UGH!**

Toilets THROUGH TIME

The next time you're crossing your legs in line for the bathroom, here's something to take your mind off your situation: The modern flush toilet has only been around since 1851. For most of human history, people had to get creative when it came to waste removal. Some ancient efforts were surprisingly clever. Others were just plain gross!

B.C.
Number One

No one is sure who invented the first toilet—probably because it's tough to tell an ancient latrine from a hole in the ground. But one early adopter was Skara Brae, a Neolithic settlement in Scotland. There, the remains of stone huts have drains extending from niches in their walls. Some historians think they were prehistoric privies.

1700 B.C.
Throne Room

The first flushable toilet hailed from the Palace of Knossos on Crete, an island in Greece. The royal throne was screened off from view and flushed by rain water from an overhead tank. Waste was sent through a sewer system that emptied through drains buried deep underground. Europe's waste systems wouldn't become that sophisticated for another 3,000 years.

| 3000 B.C. | 1700 B.C. | A.D. 1 | 300 | 600 |

A.D. 200
Public Privy

Ancient Romans were at the forefront of flushing. Their system of aqueducts carried in a flow of freshwater to fill bathing pools—and carried away waste from the toilets in the city's famed bathhouses. Romans liked to do their business in groups, sitting cheek to cheek on long benchlike latrines that could seat up to 20 at once. After they'd finished their business, they would share a stick on a sponge for wiping.

AHHH, SQUEAKY CLEAN

1000
Castle Commode

In medieval Europe, people mostly used chamber pots or a hole in the ground when they had to answer the call of nature. That changed when a castle-building boom hit in the 11th century, and new designs included indoor outhouses. Known as garderobes, they were small, bottomless rooms that stuck out from castle walls. The name is likely a shortening of "guarding one's robes," a phrase that referred to people hanging their clothes in the toilet shaft so the strong ammonia odors would kill the fleas.

TOILET BOXES ARE SO PASSÉ.

1550s
Luxe Loo

After a few centuries, garderobes fell out of fashion and were replaced by something a little simpler: a box with a lid. King Louis XI of France hid his behind curtains and used herbs to mask the odor. In England, Queen Elizabeth I had a velvet-and-lace version. But she was quick to swap it out when her godson, Sir John Harrington, invented the first modern flushing toilet.

900	1200	1500	1800	2100

1880s
Royal Flush

In the 1880s, Edward, the future king of England, hired a London plumber by the fantastically fitting name of Thomas Crapper to build bathrooms in several royal palaces. Crapper helped popularize private flushing toilets—though contrary to popular opinion, he didn't invent them. Toilet tinkerers continued to refine the design, but it hasn't changed much since. Maybe we're due for a more modern potty.

141

BEDS

A Story to **Tuck Into**

Humans have been looking for a cozy place to curl up and catch some z's for as long as we've lived on Earth. Today, people snooze on everything from memory foam to remote-controlled mattresses. But sleeping situations weren't always so cushy.

The oldest known bed was discovered in KwaZulu-Natal, South Africa. The 77,000-year-old mattress was made of layers of reeds and rushes. At 22 square feet (2 sq m), it was big enough to fit the whole family. The mattress shows evidence of being burned every so often—probably to kill pests that were living inside.

Critters were a big problem for the sleepers of yore. People eventually got the idea to raise their beds on wooden platforms—or even piles of dirt—to try and discourage creepy-crawlies from climbing under the covers with them. The ancient Egyptians were the first to invent the raised bed: The pharaoh Tutankhamun slept on one made of ebony and gold.

What's in **a Name?**

The phrase "making the bed" likely comes from the old practice of taking the stuffing out of the mattress every morning to air it out and remove pests, and then restuffing it at night.

Later, in medieval Europe, beds got a mega makeover. They became humongous—one, the Great Bed of Ware, a tourist attraction at an English inn, was more than 10 feet (3 m) wide. They were often hung with long velvet curtains and decorated with wood carvings. Back then, beds were status symbols that displayed someone's wealth and power. It was even common for people to receive guests while lounging in their bedrooms!

17TH- OR 18TH-CENTURY BED FROM ITALY

KITCHENS

A **Fireside** Story

These days, kitchens aren't just a place for cooking: They're where kids do homework, guests gather, and families come together to discuss their days over dinner. Aside from being one of the most important rooms in the house, the kitchen is likely also the oldest.

People used kitchens even before they had homes. In 2009, archaeologists in the Czech Republic discovered a prehistoric barbecue where ancient humans roasted reindeer, wolverine, and giant woolly mammoth. Even after people moved out of caves and into houses, most didn't have kitchens indoors. In ancient Rome, everyone but the wealthy waited in line to use public kitchens. Others opted not to cook at all—since the Romans were the inventors of street food, they didn't have to. People visited open-air stalls for fast-food snacks like sausages and chickpea cakes, doused in a fermented fish sauce called *garum*.

In medieval times, people finally brought their cooking fires inside. Medieval Europeans and Native Americans vented smoke through holes in their roofs. But it didn't work very well: Homes were constantly filled with thick, choking clouds. People spent a lot of their indoor time squinting and coughing until 1330, when brick fireplaces were invented. They solved the smoke problem but didn't give off much heat. People went to great lengths to keep warm: Some even built enormous fireplaces with benches installed right inside.

In the 19th century, stoves and indoor plumbing for sinks arrived on the scene. People built worktables and cabinets for storage around them, and cooked up the first modern kitchens.

Bet You **Didn't Know**

People in the Victorian era loved to cook. One recorded menu lists this dinner for six people: carrot stew, fish, lobster patties, stewed kidneys, roast lamb, boiled turkey, ham, potatoes, onions, macaroni, and two kinds of pudding.

NOW THAT'S WHAT I CALL A **HEALTHY APPETITE!**

BATHROOMS

A Story to Soak In

People have been washing up for as long as we've been around. But through history, some have definitely been better at it than others.

The ancient Romans were expert bathers. Rome's network of water-carrying aqueducts brought freshwater into huge pubic bathhouses—a lot of it. All in all, the rate at which water was delivered worked out to some 300 gallons (1,136 L) per person per day! One bathhouse, the great Baths of Caracalla, could hold 1,600 bathers at a time. Bathhouses weren't just a place to clean up: Many boasted libraries, barbers, tennis courts, and snack bars. They were such an important part of Roman life that when meeting a new acquaintance, it was common to ask where he bathed.

In the Middle Ages, things took a turn for the grimy. The outbreak of the plague led many people to mistakenly believe that water spread illness, and bathhouses fell out of fashion. In England, Queen Elizabeth I was said to have bathed only once a month "whether she needs it or no."

I'M **HONORED** BY YOUR LACK OF B.O.

CARVING OF ISIS

Bet You Didn't Know

In many cultures, bathing has religious significance. The ancient Egyptians bathed twice a day to honor the goddess Isis.

People didn't come around to the idea of getting wet again until the 16th century, when vacationers to the town of Bath, England, started taking cautious dunks in the local hot springs. When they didn't get sick and die, they decided maybe bathing wasn't so bad after all.

Over time, people decided that bathing kept them healthy. Victorian-era bathers thought the more uncomfortable their technique, the better: They often plunged into icy water. And one early Victorian shower had such powerful pressure that people had to strap on protective headgear before stepping in!

BRING IT ON, WATER.

147

TREE
HOUSES

The **High** Life

Tree houses make perfect forts, clubhouses, and sleepover spots. But did you know that they have a long history as permanent homes?

In some parts of the world, treetop living just makes sense. Tree houses were once common dwellings in Southeast Asia and the South Pacific. Homes high off the ground kept people safe from floods, protected them from wild animals, and brought them closer to light and air in the middle of the dark jungle. To come and go, they would step inside a basket, which could be raised and lowered with a pulley system.

In the 17th century, British explorer Captain James Cook visited Tasmania, Australia, where he saw local people living in tree houses. When he went home and reported what he'd seen, people went crazy for the idea.

Queen Elizabeth I had a three-story dwelling built in the branches of a lime tree. Many English tree houses were attached to their trees with rope. They'd be tied on every summer and then taken down in the winter, so the tree had a chance to grow.

In 19th-century France, a chestnut-tree-lined street in the town of Plessis-Robinson became famous for its treetop restaurants. Hip Parisians traveled there to dine on roast chicken and champagne that was hoisted up from ground level in baskets. You might call it *tree chic!*

TREE HOUSE CAFÉ IN PARIS

Bet You **Didn't Know**

The world's tallest tree house, in Crossville, Tennessee, U.S.A., has more than 80 rooms, a crow's nest, and a bell tower.

WELCOME **Home**

Opening the front door and entering your home at the end of a long day is a comforting feeling. But as well as you think you know your house, it's hiding a lot of history.

Front Door

Experts think the first front doors didn't offer a lot of security: They were just a screen or branches or an animal hide. Heavy stone doors came next, and they offered serious protection—but they were tough to crack open to see if the person knocking was a friend or foe.

HALT!
STATE YOUR BUSINESS!

Peephole

People eventually started cutting slits in their doors so they could see out, but that meant that dangerous things—like fire, poison, or arrows—could get in. They replaced slits with tiny doors at eye level to peep through. Today, peepholes let someone see who's at the door without being seen themselves.

Lawn

When settlers first immigrated to America from England, they longed for the rolling lawns they had left behind. They had to experiment to find grass that would grow in the New World, and then they had to water it by hand since they didn't have the right humid, rainy conditions. Over time, Americans got creative with lawn upkeep—U.S. president Woodrow Wilson kept a herd of sheep to keep the White House lawn under control.

Garage

Today, people are just as likely to use their garage for storing holiday decorations, piles of papers, and old toys as they are for parking a car. But when cars were first invented, they weren't very sturdy: If a Model T got rained on, it might need a new engine. The first garages were converted carriage houses, and many people parked the family car right alongside their horses.

Porch

Porches seem as American as apple pie. But they actually originated in ancient Greece, from the porticoes that decorated temple entrances. And in the days before air conditioning, porches weren't just a place to relax: People used these shady retreats to escape from the heat.

CHAPTER 7

Sports & Enter- tainment

The next time you're scarfing down peanuts at a ball game, cheering on the underdog, or giving your all to your team, consider this: Sports have been around for thousands of years. Some of the sports in this chapter have origins in warfare; others were born out of boredom. And your favorite just may have a wacky back-story you've never heard.

FOOTBALL

Game On

I GOT IT!

There's no question that football is a physical sport. Players get pounded as they scramble to gain yards and as enormous defenders deliver unforgiving tackles. But as violent as America's favorite sport seems, it's got nothing on the ancient games it evolved from.

Around 2000 B.C., the ancient Greeks invented a ball game called *episkyros*. No one is sure what the rules were, but since the balls were made of linen and wrapped in hair, they didn't bounce very well. That leads experts to believe they were tossed and carried instead. One thing they do know: Both men and women were involved, and they always played naked. Hey, no sweaty uniforms to wash!

By the Middle Ages, the British were playing mellay, a game that involved large numbers of people trying to punch, throw, or carry an air-filled animal bladder. Contests could involve hundreds of players, all kicking each other in the shins and flinging people to the ground. Goals were about half a mile (0.8 km) apart—about seven times farther apart than a modern American football field—so the bloodshed could go on for hours between points.

In the 1820s, football evolved into two distinct sports: soccer and rugby. In America, these two sports also recombined to form a brand-new one, which got its start on college campuses around 1870: American football. By the early 1900s, the sport had formalized rules, but games were still incredibly dangerous. In the 1905 season, football racked up 149 serious injuries and 18 deaths. President Theodore Roosevelt called for reform, leading to the creation of the National Collegiate Athletic Association (NCAA), and safer rules along with it. Football went pro in 1922 with the founding of the National Football League (NFL). The modern—and thankfully less bloody—sport was born.

Bet You **Didn't Know**

The football huddle was invented in the 1890s by quarterback Paul Hubbard, a player at a college for the deaf who was frustrated that the other team—also made up of deaf players—could read the sign language he was using to call plays.

GOALIE MASKS

Facing Danger

Bet You **Didn't Know**

The National Hockey League still does not have an official rule requiring goalies to wear masks.

On November 1, 1959, a flying puck struck Montreal Canadiens goalie Jacques Plante in the face. Plante got stitched up and then returned to the ice wearing a new accessory—a fiberglass mask.

Plante's protective gear earned him jeers at the game. Despite the fact that a slap shot can send a frozen puck flying at more than 100 miles an hour (161 km/h), no player had ever worn a mask on the ice before.

Canadiens coach Tom Blake worried the mask would keep his goalie from being able to see the puck—and that it might make his team look like a bunch of wimps. He wanted Plante to ditch the mask after his stitches came out, but Plante had had enough. He refused to lace up his skates if he couldn't wear his mask. Plante convinced his coach—and then likely everyone else—that the headgear didn't interfere with his playing when the Canadiens won their next 18 games in a row. He got to keep his mask.

Hockey players pride themselves on being tough, so it took 15 more years before all goaltenders agreed to safety and masked up. By then, goalies had started decorating their masks with scary artwork meant to intimidate their opponents. During the 1970s, every time the Boston Bruins' Gerry Cheevers got hit in the face, his trainer would draw a line of stitches on his mask to mark the spot. More recently, goalie Thomas Greiss used a mask decorated with the gaping jaws of a great white shark—in honor of his then team, the San Jose Sharks. Imagine trying to score against that beast of the deep!

THOMAS GREISS

REFEREES

Keeping the **Peace**

*LET THE GAMES **BEGIN**, OLD CHAPS!*

Before the first referees of modern times started blowing their whistles on the field, there was no one to keep players in line. For ages it was assumed that no gentleman would ever bend the rules to score a point or— *gasp!*—foul another player on purpose.

It took modern sports organizations until the 19th century to realize that players can't always be trusted when the game is on the line. In the 1840s, football (or soccer, as Americans would say) teams in the United Kingdom nominated umpires— one for each team—to make sure players followed the rules. But these officials were often biased toward the team they represented, so a third party was needed to "referee" when they disagreed.

In the early days of American football, referees wore white dress shirts, bow ties, and beret-style hats. People thought that formal dress would give them an air of authority. But since some teams also wore white, the getup made it hard to tell the referees apart from the players. (Also, they looked pretty silly.)

When a quarterback accidentally passed the ball to a referee named Lloyd Olds during a 1920 football game, Olds decided something finally had to be done. He asked a friend to make him a shirt that would stand out on the field. The resulting black-and-white-striped garment was hard to miss. Fans booed the first time he wore it, but the design worked—and has stuck around ever since.

Bet You **Didn't Know**

When color TV was first introduced in the 1960s, football referees briefly sported shirts decorated in bright red and white stripes.

BASKETBALL

Boredom **Buster**

SWISH?

Bet You **Didn't Know**

At first, basketball team sizes were flexible so everyone could play. Some games had more than 100 players battling for the ball!

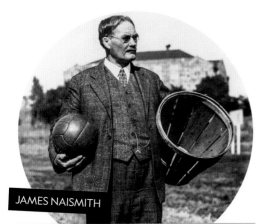

JAMES NAISMITH

Today, millions of fans watch their favorite professional athletes dunk and dribble on TV, and millions more take to the basketball court themselves. It's one of the most popular sports in the world. And it all started with some bored kids.

In December 1891, James Naismith, a physical education instructor at the International Y.M.C.A. Training School in Springfield, Massachusetts, U.S.A., was out of ideas. His class of track and field runners was stuck indoors for the winter, and they were tired of jumping jacks and push-ups. So Naismith got creative. He nailed two peach baskets to the gymnasium wall, grabbed a soccer ball, and scribbled down the basic rules of a new game: basketball.

In its early days, basketball was kind of a slow sport: Every time a player scored, the action had to stop while someone fetched a ladder to retrieve the ball from the basket. Finally, someone thought to cut a hole in the bottom of the basket—but they only made it big enough for a bystander wielding a long pole to poke the ball out from the bottom. It wasn't until 1912 that the baskets were swapped out for nets that allowed the ball to swish though.

Basketball became really big in the 1980s, when superstar players like Magic Johnson and Michael Jordan wowed audiences with their aerial acrobatics—and ignited a world-wide craze for the sport.

MICHAEL JORDAN

Winston

BULLS
23

ROBERTSON
21

MASCOTS

Team mascots—whether birds of prey, wild animals, or made-up creatures—are a key part of the game. But if you think about it, having someone dance around in a silly suit cheering for a team is pretty strange. So how did they get their start?

I STRIKE FEAR INTO THE HEARTS OF VISITING TEAMS!

HANDSOME DAN

The idea for American sports team mascots can be traced all the way back to a French opera called *La Mascotte* that was popular in the 1880s. It tells the story of a struggling farmer whose life takes a turn for the better after he is visited by a mystical being named Bettina. Apparently not realizing the word *mascotte* is a play on French slang for "witch," American fans thought using a magical being to bring their team good luck seemed worth trying. So they started bringing live animals to games. At the very least, the barks, snorts, and roars probably intimidated their team's opponents!

162

PHILLIE PHANATIC

Some mascots took on a life of their own. In 1974, a San Diego radio station hired local college student Ted Giannoulas to dress up in a chicken suit and promote the Padres baseball team. The Padres were terrible. But the chicken was so entertaining that people started going to the games just to watch the fowl play. When the radio station fired Giannoulas, he bought his own chicken suit and kept right on shaking his tail feathers.

WHAT ARE YOU ... CHICKEN?

Bet You Didn't Know

The Philadelphia Phillies' mascot, the Phillie Phanatic, was created by the same puppet designer who created the Muppet Miss Piggy.

Soon, anyone or anything that was nearby when a team started doing well was called a mascot. The Harvard baseball team adopted John the Orangeman, a bearded fruit seller who happened to hawk his produce during a lucky streak. To this day, Yale University has Handsome Dan, a bulldog that walks the field before games.

Ancient Sports:
EXTREME EDITION

Think snowboarding and skydiving are extreme? Ancient athletes would have scoffed. These bloody, no-holds-barred games from history will leave you running for your pads and helmet.

1500 B.C.
Heads Up

No one is sure exactly what the rules were in Mexico's ancient sport now called the Mesoamerican ball game, but experts think it was something like volleyball without a net. Players wearing protective padding used their hips to hit a heavy rubber ball weighing in at about 10 pounds (4.5 kg). The Aztec added an especially violent twist: Some depictions show that they beheaded the losing team—then used the decapitated heads in place of the ball at the next match.

1500 B.C.	1000	500	A.D. 1	500

648 B.C.
Fatal Fight

An extreme combination of boxing and wrestling called *pankration* was first introduced at the 33rd Olympic Games in ancient Greece. There were only two rules: No biting and no gouging out your opponent's eyes. There was no time limit, and the fight didn't end until someone was knocked out or raised his index finger to signal defeat. Ancient Greeks must have been tough because many died instead of giving up.

185 B.C.
Beastly Battle

Being a gladiator was not for the fainthearted. Imagine sparring with a warrior armed to the teeth, intent on killing you or dying in the attempt. Now imagine that warrior was a mighty African elephant. In ancient Rome, fighters called *venatores* faced off against lions, tigers, bears, crocodiles, and even elephants. Some gladiators wore suits of armor, but others had only leather bands on their arms and legs for protection.

46 B.C
Sea Skirmish

Ancient Romans take the trophy for history's most violent sports. When they weren't watching gladiators, another popular pastime was the spectacle known as the naumachia—a mock naval battle. Staged in specially built man-made lakes or flooded amphitheaters, fleets of ships went to battle. But there was nothing staged about the results: Hundreds of convicts went to a watery death during these events.

TODAY
Stick It to Me

It might sound too deadly for today, but the ancient martial art called *intonga*, also called stick fighting, still exists. This South African sport has been practiced for thousands of years, and seems to be making a comeback. Wielding three sticks of different lengths, competitors whack away at each other to prove their fighting mettle.

1000   1500   2000   MODERN DAY

1000
Viking vs. Viking

Today, tug-of-war is a harmless group game. But its origins were a little more extreme: Ancient Vikings, known for their great size, strength, and fighting skills, liked to play games as a form of battle practice. Using a rope made of stitched-together animal skins, two teams would face off—over an open pit of fire. The losers burned to death, and the winners claimed their belongings.

Bet You **Didn't Know**

Skateboarding becomes an Olympic sport for the first time at the 2020 Summer Games in Tokyo, Japan.

SKATEBOARDS

A Wild **Ride**

Surfing first splashed onto California's beach scene in the 1950s. Before long, it seemed like everyone was paddling out to ride the waves. But what were they supposed to do when the surf was down?

Shore-bound surfers came up with the idea to attach metal roller skate wheels to wooden boards so they could surf the sidewalk. Almost overnight, long-haired, sandal-clad surfers were riding the concrete all over California's beach towns. By 1963, companies were manufacturing boards and hosting competitions. But early skateboarders weren't doing tricks. Instead, they "freestyled"—kind of like dancing on wheels.

In 1965, the skateboarding trend crashed. Most people thought that "sidewalk surfing" was simply a fad whose end had come, and skateboard companies went out of business overnight. Then, in 1973, skateboarding zoomed back on the scene.

The invention of wheels made of polyurethane, a type of plastic, meant that a once teeth-chattering ride became relatively smooth. The wheels had better grip, too, which meant, for the first time, skaters could roll up banks and down ditches.

In 1976, California was in the midst of a drought. To save water, homeowners drained their swimming pools—and those giant empty holes turned out to be the perfect place to develop skateboarding tricks. Armed with loads of new moves, including kickflips and ollies, skateboarders returned to the streets. Today, they're still sliding down handrails and flying off ramps. Some even go pro and earn money with their fancy footwork.

DON'T TRY THIS AT HOME!

SWIM
FINS

Many colonial-era Americans preferred to stay safely on dry land. But not Benjamin Franklin. As a kid, the future Founding Father loved to swim and even dreamed of sailing the high seas.

Long before he helped write the Declaration of Independence or experimented with electricity, Franklin was inventing all kinds of things. One of these creations was a set of swim fins made of wood, which he designed when he was just 11 years old. Shaped like lily pads, they attached to his hands and helped propel him through the water. When his wrists tired out, he tried strapping the fins to his feet instead.

168

GOT MY GEAR ON, LET'S **ROLL OUT!**

problem: leftover naval mines hidden underwater in areas like Normandy, France. To clear the explosive devices, the Navy deployed special soldiers nicknamed the Naked Warriors because they wore no uniform, just swim trunks, a snorkeling mask, and swim fins to help them speed through the water. Today, swim fins can be found on dive boats, at pools, and on the feet of snorkelers at beaches around the world.

Modern swim fins, sometimes called flippers, didn't surface until much later, in 1940. Their inventor was an American gold medal yacht racer named Owen P. Churchill, who found inspiration for his design when he traveled to Tahiti in the South Pacific. There, he saw young boys weaving mats, attaching metal straps to them, then dipping the whole contraption in tar. After the tar hardened, the boys attached these homemade swim fins to their feet.

Churchill went home and made his own version of the fins out of rubber, but they didn't sell well. That changed after World War II, when the U.S. Navy faced a new

Bet You **Didn't Know**

A new kind of single swim fin shaped like a dolphin's tail allows swimmers to reach speeds nearly twice that of Olympian Michael Phelps.

NOISEMAKERS

When soccer fans entered Portland, Oregon, U.S.A.'s Civic Stadium for the World Cup qualifying game on September 7, 1997, they were handed something strange: a pair of long balloons made of thick plastic.

At first, many didn't know what the balloons were for. But someone figured out that banging them together made a surprisingly loud clapping noise. Other fans caught on fast, and soon the crowd was really amped up. One player later reported, "The stadium sounded like it was going to fall down." Today, the balloons, now called ThunderStix, can be seen—and heard—at major sporting events all over the world.

But noisemakers aren't a new idea. Experts know that ancient people had noisemakers such as bone whistles for sacred rites. And militaries have long used horns and drums to make their armies sound more imposing.

THUNDERSTIX

Fast-forward to modern times, and noise-makers have a long history not just as a cheering aid—but as a major annoyance. People started banging cowbells at college football games in the late 1930s, leading the Southeastern Conference to ban all artificial noisemakers. Plastic horns called vuvuzelas made a loud entrance at the 2010 soccer World Cup. Some fans loved their power: At 127 decibels, they were louder than a chain saw. Others longed for a little peace and quiet: South African shopkeepers reported running out of special ear plugs called Vuvu-Stops.

Bet You Didn't Know

It is believed that the vuvuzela originated from a traditional horn called a kudu that was blown to summon African villagers to meetings.

VUVUZELA

ROLLER SKATES

The **Wheel** Story

I n 1760, a London inventor named Joseph Merlin decided he wanted to make a grand entrance at a party. He designed a pair of boots equipped with two in-line wheels each, slipped them on his feet, and rolled in to the festivities while playing a violin. He probably should have done a test run first.

Merlin hadn't outfitted his invention with a way to turn or brake, so he fiddled his way right into a full-length mirror. Merlin's violin—and probably his pride—was severely damaged.

Creating skates that could turn was a big roadblock for early inventors. Their designs attached the wheels directly to the sole of the skate, which meant they could only roll straight ahead. That changed in 1863, when a New York City furniture maker named James L. Plimpton had the idea to put the wheels on a separate piece that would attach to the skate with a pivoting mechanism.

For the first time, skaters could turn by shifting their weight. Plimpton converted the dining room of a local hotel into the world's first roller rink.

Roller-skating whizzed from popular pastime to national obsession in the 1950s. Drive-in restaurants put waitresses on skates to speed up delivery of burgers and fries to diners waiting outside in their cars. And the creation of Roller Derby saw teams (usually all-female) zooming around oval tracks and trying to stop opponents from passing—using any means necessary. Today, Roller Derby is one of the fastest growing sports in the world.

Bet You **Didn't Know**

The first wedding on roller skates took place in 1912.

STRANGE **Stadiums**

A baseball field seems pretty standard—by rule, it has to be a square, 90 feet (27.4 m) on each side, with the pitcher's mound exactly 60.5 feet (18.4 m) from home plate. But as long as they meet the regulations, stadiums are free to add their own unique twist. Throughout baseball history, some stadiums in the United States have really hit it out of the park.

Playing Hardball

For nearly 50 years, from 1928 to 1975, fielding was not for the fainthearted at the University of Texas at Austin. The baseball team played with a cliff right in the middle of their field. Construction crews had blasted away a slope when building Clark Field—but they never finished the job. To snag a fly ball, players had to dash up a path called Billy Goat Trail.

Out of Left Field

When the Dodgers moved from Brooklyn, New York, to Los Angeles in 1958, their stadium was still under construction. In the meantime, the Dodgers played at the Los Angeles Memorial Coliseum. One problem: The stadium was designed for football. Left field was only 250 feet (76.2 m) long—making almost any fly ball hit to the left an automatic home run.

Moving Target

Hitting a homer was nearly impossible at Cleveland Municipal Stadium, the former home of Ohio's Cleveland Indians: The centerfield fence measured a distant 463 feet (141 m) from home plate. So owner Bill Veeck got creative: He installed a movable fence. Depending on the skill set of their opponent, the team could shrink or expand the field by as much as 15 feet (4.5 m).

Fly Ball

Putting a roof on a baseball stadium to keep out the weather might seem like a good idea. But it didn't work out that way at the Minnesota Twins' Hubert H. Humphrey Metrodome, the team's stadium from 1982 to 2009. Balls were constantly bouncing off its roof and ricocheting out of play. On May 4, 1980, Minnesota player Dave Kingsman managed to hit a ball into a drainage hole and it never came down.

CHAPTER 8

Beauty, Hygiene & Medicine

Every morning, we stand in front of the mirror, washing, brushing, and primping. We humans have been sprucing ourselves up since we climbed out of our caves and noticed we were a little ... grimy. On our quest to look our best, we've come up with all kinds of concoctions. Some were brilliant, but others were disgusting, dangerous, or just plain duds.

SOAP

Coming Clean

There's no cleaning creation used more than soap—we wash up with it several times a day (hopefully)! But what's the story behind this sudsy stuff?

The first cleansing agents came from plants. In the second millennium B.C., the Hittites, an ancient people who ruled an empire in what is now Turkey, burned the soapwort plant—which contains a natural cleanser called saponin—and combined the ashes with water, then washed with it. Not everyone saw the appeal. Early Greeks opted to scrape oil and dirt off their skin with a metal instrument called a strigil. Sounds relaxing!

By about 600 B.C., the Phoenicians, a Mediterranean seafaring people most famous for inventing the alphabet, figured out how to boil ashes, water, and goat fat together to make a waxy substance that removed dirt.

SOAPWORT

PHOENICIAN STATUE

178

They didn't understand the chemistry, but they had created a recipe for soap. The substance attached to grime and grit on the body and suspended it in suds, which could then be washed away.

By A.D. 800, soapmaking had become an art. Soapmakers added exotic fragrances and oils that made sudsing up a more enjoyable experience. But soap didn't become an everyday item until the Crimean War of the 1850s. Back then, more soldiers died from disease than battle wounds. So when they started using soap—and stopped dying in droves—people noticed. Soldiers brought their new fondness for scrubbing up home from the war, and the habit stuck.

YOU'RE WELCOME!

What's in **a Name?**

The term "soap opera" comes from the early 1900s, when a soap manufacturer flooded daytime radio dramas with so many commercials that the shows got a new nickname.

LIPSTICK

PUCKER UP!

Did you know some lipsticks contain fish scales? They're added to boost shine. If that seems gross, you might want to brace yourself. The ingredients of many ancient lipsticks weren't just strange—they were downright dangerous.

The first documented lip tint, worn by a Sumerian queen in 2500 B.C., contained lead, a substance that can be poisonous, even deadly if a person is exposed to too much of it. Ancient Greeks used cinnabar, a type of mercury that tinted their lips a lovely shade of red—but also shortened their life spans.

180

white—the better to set off her crimson pout. The queen was such a devotee of lip color that she believed it had healing powers and even the ability to ward off death. That's a bit ironic, considering toxic lead was almost certainly one of the ingredients in her lipstick. Since then, red lipstick has become an iconic statement of female power. Bonus: It's no longer deadly!

Bet You Didn't Know

Both men and women in ancient Egypt wore red lipstick as a status symbol.

Other lipstick ingredients weren't toxic, but modern people might still hesitate to put them on their faces: Ancient Egyptians made lip colors from crushed ants and beetles; ancient Greeks sometimes made theirs from crocodile feces and sheep sweat. (Sadly, history doesn't tell us how these people collected these ingredients.)

One of history's most famous lipstick-wearers was Queen Elizabeth I: She painted her lips bright red and powdered her face

THIS SHADE IS **TO DIE FOR.**

QUEEN ELIZABETH I

NAIL POLISH

Finger **Painting**

There's no part of the body humans haven't tried to adorn, from the tops of our heads all the way to the tips of our fingers and toes. But who were the first people to decide their digits deserved decorating?

The original nail-painters weren't women; they were male warriors. About 5,000 years ago, Babylonian fighters indulged in a prebattle ritual of primping and preening. They got their hair curled, their lips tinted, and their nails shaped and colored before heading off to fight.

The first nail paint was developed in China around 3000 B.C. and was made of beeswax, egg white, tree sap, and gelatin. Dyes made from vegetables added color. Nail polish was a way to show off social status: Only Chinese royals were allowed to sport flashy colors like gold and silver. If a peasant with an eye for the shiny glint of metal used one of those, the punishment was death.

As centuries passed, people continued the manicure habit. But until the early 20th century, nail polish was only available in cake, paste, powder, or stick form. Then, in 1914, European chemists hit on a new invention: a compound called nitrocellulose. It was used to make gunpowder during World War I, and after the fighting stopped, chemists discovered they could add it to paint to make a durable, waterproof finish. It wasn't long before it became an ingredient in nail polish. It can still be found adorning fingers and toes today—until it chips off, that is.

DO I LOOK BATTLE-READY?

Bet You **Didn't Know**

Cleopatra was famous for her signature deep-red manicure.

PERFUME

A Worldwide **Scent-sation**

184

There's no question that the olden days were pretty stinky. During the Middle Ages, churches across Europe actually discouraged people from bathing. Authorities thought a good scrub spread disease, believing that water carried sickness into the body through the skin. (Sounds like someone really wanted to get out of bath time!)

Bet You **Didn't Know**

Researchers are trying to re-create a perfume from traces of a 3,500-year-old scent that might once have been worn by the Egyptian female pharaoh Hatshepsut.

As a result, people avoided washing like, well, the plague. Even the finicky upper class only risked it a few times a year. Queen Isabella I of Spain reportedly bathed only twice in her life—once when she was born and again when she got married.

So the odors of yesteryear were pretty intense. How did people live with them?

JUST AVOID **DEEP BREATHS!**

QUEEN ISABELLA I OF SPAIN

More than 8,000 years ago, incense spiked with the aromatic tree resins frankincense and myrrh, along with cinnamon, was burned at religious ceremonies—probably to mask the smell of sacrificed animals. The ancient Egyptians were big fans of perfume: They wore cones of perfumed fat atop their heads, which would melt in the summer heat and drench them with sweet-smelling oil.

Perfumes were made with oil until the Middle Ages, when it was discovered that certain animal products could carry scents with less mess. One of these, ambergris, forms in the intestines of sperm whales. This "gold of the sea" is considered more valuable than gold today, but the United States bans its use in perfumes to protect sperm whales, which are an endangered species. Thankfully for both whales and our noses, perfumers figured out how to create lasting scents with artificial ingredients.

NAIL CLIPPERS

Keeping **Trim**

Nail clippers aren't exactly the best designed invention. The clamp isn't long enough to fit an entire nail, and each snip sends overgrown bits flying into the dark corners of the bathroom. But did you know that until fairly recently, humans didn't have a dedicated tool for trimming their nails at all?

In ancient times, many people avoided cutting their fingernails in the first place. During the rule of China's Ming dynasty, from 1368 to 1644, long fingernails were a sign of high status. They showed that a person was wealthy enough to avoid nail-breaking manual labor. Some people even wore elaborate nail covers to keep them protected.

But those who had to do their own farming, cooking, and cleaning needed a way to keep their digits ready for work. Before nail clippers were invented, people didn't cut their nails. Instead, they used a knife to pare them down—a bit like peeling an apple!

Amazingly, no one created an implement for the job until the late 19th century, when the first patents for nail clippers began to appear. These days, most clippers operate on the same principle: A lever squeezes a bladed clamp around the nail until it is severed. But that hasn't stopped intrepid entrepreneurs from trying to nail new designs. One pair of toenail clippers has extra-long handles so users don't have to contort themselves to reach their feet.

NAILED IT

Bet You **Didn't Know**

A superstition popular in the late 1800s warned that cutting your fingernails on the weekend would bring bad luck.

INSIDE THE DOCTOR'S Office

Have you ever been waiting for your doctor in an exam room and passed the time by checking out all the strange tools and equipment in there? Here's the lowdown on some of the devices you might have seen.

YOU'VE GOT THE BEAT!

Adhesive Bandages

In 1920, Johnson & Johnson employee Earle Dickson was puzzling over a problem: His wife, Josephine, was always nicking her fingers in the kitchen. He would wrap her wounds in gauze and pieces of adhesive tape, but the process was clumsy. His idea? Dickson laid a narrow strip of gauze down the center of a roll of adhesive tape, then put a piece of fabric on top to cover the sticky parts. The next time Josephine cut herself, she could simply pull off the fabric and use the prepared tape. The ready-made bandage was born.

Stethoscope

Doctors have long listened to the heart's sounds to diagnose problems. But putting your ear against someone's chest to hear the beat is impractical—not to mention awkward. In 1816, French physician René Laënnec had an aha moment. He asked for a piece of paper, rolled it into a tube, and pressed it to a patient's chest. Laënnec was excited to discover that the heartbeat was amplified through the tube. Though as an accomplished flute player, perhaps he already had an inkling that his idea would work.

Cotton Swabs

In 1923, new father Leo Gerstenzang was alarmed when he saw his wife using a toothpick stuck into a wad of cotton to clean their baby's ears. He set about coming up with a safer version: a stick with blunt ends and cotton that wouldn't fall off. With his new product, he founded what would become Q-tips, Inc. Ironically, today doctors warn that cotton swabs should never be used for cleaning out the ears—35 people a day end up in emergency rooms after injuring themselves that way.

Eye Chart

Anyone who's ever squinted their way through an eye test will recognize this chart of letters that grow smaller from top to bottom. A French doctor named Ferdinand Monoyer invented it in 1872. Each row of letters represents a different diopter—a unit of measurement for vision. If you ignore the bottom row and read the letters on the edges upward from the bottom, you'll notice that the inventor wrote his name into his creation.

D:5m

5 M R T V F U E N C X O Z D 1,0

5,55 D L V A T B K U E H S N 0,9

6,25 R C Y H O F M E S P A 0,8

7,14 E X A T Z H D W N 0,7

8,33 Y O E L K S F D I 0,6

10 O X P H B Z D 0,5

12,50 N L T A V R 0,4

16,66 O H S U E 0,3

25 M C F 0,2

50 Z U 0,1

HAIR DYE

Locks to Love

Bet You **Didn't Know**

Some ancient Europeans, known as the Saxons, colored their hair bright red, green, orange, and sky blue to intimidate opponents on the battlefield.

Having a bad hair day? You're not alone—people have been getting the urge to change up their dos since the dawn of time.

Ancient civilizations were dabbling in hair dye as far back as 1500 B.C. Egyptians used henna, a reddish brown dye made from plants, to conceal graying strands. In Greece, long, light-colored curls were in fashion. People would get the look by sitting in the sunlight to lighten their locks. Some would speed up the process by sprinkling pollen, flour, or even gold dust in their hair. How fancy! Over in Rome, dark tendrils were trendy. Ancient hairdressers invented a permanent black hair dye, but when it was discovered to be toxic, they switched to a formula made with leeches that had been fermented in a lead container for two months. How ... unusual?

It wasn't until the mid-1800s that someone figured out how to make a synthetic hair dye. English chemist William Henry Perkin was trying to make a malaria drug when he accidentally created a mauve-colored dye instead. The molecule responsible, para-phenylenediamine, is still the foundation of many hair dyes today.

Early hair dyes were not for the faint-hearted: Because many formulations included harsh chemicals, women often walked out of the beauty shop with blistered foreheads and swollen eyelids. But chemists improved their formulas over time. By 1968, so many women dyed their tresses that U.S. passports stopped listing hair color—what was the point? At first, hair dyeing was seen as something to hide: Women colored their hair at home, in secret. But dye lost its taboo, and today, both men and women sport all sorts of shades, from blonde to blue.

DID SOMEONE SAY MY NAME?

LEECH

HAIR **DRYER**

OH MY!

Before the blow dryer was invented in the 1920s, people had to get creative if they didn't want to leave the house with dripping tresses.

The hair drying devices of yore didn't work that well. One was a brush filled with boiling water people (carefully!) combed through their locks around 1880. Around the same time, a French stylist named Alexandre-Ferdinand Godefroy invented a "hair dressing device" that heated air with a gas stove, then sent it blowing through a tube into a large bonnet. Back then, fashionable ladies wore their hair in elaborate updos, festooned with ribbons, feathers, and flowers.

Since Godefroy's device didn't circulate air well, it didn't cut their drying time by much. So in the early 20th century, many women used something they already had on hand: the vacuum cleaner. If that sounds painful, don't worry: Women would attach special hair-drying hoses to their vacuums' exhaust, switch the machine on, and blow their locks dry.

DIDN'T SEE THAT COMING, **DID YOU?**

The world didn't get a workable handheld hair dryer until 1920. The problem was finding a small enough motor. Some inventors in Racine, Wisconsin, U.S.A., experimented with using one from an electric blender. Unfortunately, the dryer's metal frame overheated easily, and it was so heavy some models came with stands so users could give their arms a break. Between the 1930s and the 1950s, many women didn't style their own dos, instead visiting salons for a weekly "wash and set" underneath hood dryers. By the 1960s, handheld dryers swapped heavy metal for much lighter materials, and the designs have only heated up from there.

Bet You **Didn't Know**

Hair dryers marketed for men first popped up in the 1960s, when the mop-headed Beatles made longer locks trendy.

TOILET PAPER

Getting on **a Roll**

OUR **SAVIOR**

For thousands of years, people simply reached for what was close at hand to clean themselves up after answering the call of nature. Before the advent of indoor plumbing, since they were literally *in* nature, that meant people used moss, leaves, grass, hay, snow, or even corncobs. *Ouch!*

Some civilizations got a little more sophisticated, but their cleanup methods still seem shockingly unsanitary today. The ancient Romans dipped sponges on a stick into a bucket of salt water—then put them back in the bucket for the next user. *Ewww.*

When newspapers and magazines became common around the 18th century, people discovered they were perfect not only for reading in the bathroom, but also for wiping with after they finished their, umm, article. In 1857, a New Yorker named Joseph Gayetty tried selling sheets of hemp infused with aloe specifically for bathroom use. But Americans didn't understand why they would pay for something special when they could use any old paper for free, and the idea was a flop.

By the end of the 19th century, many homes had indoor plumbing for the first time—and people were discovering that magazines and corncobs weren't practical for their new pipes. They needed toilet paper. But many were embarrassed to ask for it at the store. Manufacturers were stumped about how to sell something people were too bashful to buy—until 1928, when the Hoberg Paper Company hit on a new strategy. They put a beautiful woman on the logo of a toilet paper brand called Charmin and advertised the product's softness, instead of what it was for. To this day, adorable babies and cuddly bears still do the work of selling toilet paper.

HUSH, WE NEED NOT SPEAK OF ONES AND TWOS!

Bet You **Didn't Know**

The average American uses 57 squares of toilet paper a day.

DEODORANT

There's no way to cover it up—people used to stink. Some scientists think prehistoric people smelled so bad it actually helped humans survive. Anthropologist Louis Leakey theorized our prehistoric body odor was so awful it stopped hungry predators in their tracks.

Some ancient people tried to mask the odor with perfume. The Egyptians took scented baths to try and stave off odors. The Romans went a step further: They perfumed their pets.

Deodorant, which eliminates stinky body smells by killing the bacteria that cause the odor, debuted in 1888. But during the buttoned-up and formal Victorian era, people were too shy to talk about bodily functions, so hardly anyone even knew the product existed.

PEE-EW! I'M HUNGRY, BUT I'M **NOT DESPERATE!**

Deodorant's big break came in 1912, when Edna Murphey, a high school student in Cincinnati, Ohio, U.S.A., debuted a new anti-odor product named Odorono ("Odor? Oh no!"). Her father, a surgeon, had invented an antiperspirant to keep his hands from sweating during surgery. Murphey discovered it worked on underarms, too. She marketed Odorono at an exposition in Atlantic City, New Jersey, U.S.A., one summer—and fortunately for her, the weather was hot. Sweaty attendees gave Odorono a whirl, and antiperspirants took off. Today, much like in ancient Rome, there are even deodorants for dogs!

ODORONO CREAM
SAFELY STOPS PERSPIRATION
1 TO 3 DAYS

AND THIS IS WHY...
* WON'T IRRITATE SKIN
* WON'T ROT CLOTHES
* NON-GREASY—VANISHES
* NON-GRITTY—VELVET SOFT
* NO WAITING TO DRY
* SAFE RIGHT AFTER SHAVING

* 50% MORE FOR YOUR MONEY THAN OTHER LEADING CREAMS

The Odorono Co., Inc., New York

ALL THIS FOR ONLY 39¢
PLUS TAX

ODO·RO·DO

Tooth Care THROUGH TIME

People may love their cars and cell phones, but when researchers quizzed Americans about the one invention they couldn't live without, the answer was the simple toothbrush. The quest for fresh breath is nothing new: People have been swishing, brushing, and spitting since the beginning of civilization.

WELL I **WAS** HAVING A GOOD HAIR DAY ...

5000 B.C.
Powder Power
The world's first toothpaste wasn't paste at all: Ancient Egyptians mixed ground ox hooves into ash and combined it with eggshell fragments, pumice stone, and a type of tree resin called myrrh. Experts think that they didn't use brushes, but instead dipped a finger in the powder and rubbed it on their teeth. Research shows that the concoction was surprisingly effective.

A.D. 1400
Brush Off
The first real toothbrush, with bristles on one end, was invented in China. People plucked stiff, spiky hairs out of hogs' necks and attached them to a handle made of bamboo or bone. The idea caught on: During the Middle Ages, Europeans made toothbrushes with horsehair bristles. Since horsehair is soft, the toothbrushes probably didn't work as well as the original design.

| 5000 B.C. | 3000 | A.D. 1 | 1400 | 1500 |

3000 B.C.
Branch Out
The oldest oral hygiene device on record hails from ancient Babylonia. Back then, people broke twigs off trees and chewed on the ends until they frayed. These DIY toothbrushes could then be scrubbed across the teeth. Ancient people favored branches that smelled and tasted good, like those from licorice trees. Some twigs had one sharpened end to use as a pick.

WE'RE COMING FOR YOU, **PLAQUE!**

The first mass-produced toothbrush got started in an unlikely place: While in prison in 1770, William Addis was grossed out by the rags given to convicts for teeth cleaning. He begged for hair bristles from a prison guard, somehow managed to drill holes in a small animal bone, and put it all together to make a toothbrush. Once he was released, Addis founded a successful toothbrush manufacturing company.

1780
Prison to Profit

1935
Fresh Update

A research team at the DuPont Company was on the hunt for a synthetic super-material to function as a substitute for silk. They hit on nylon. Tough and lightweight, nylon was first used in the manufacture of parachutes during World War II. Over time, it made its way into toothbrushes, replacing animal-hair bristles with synthetic ones.

| 1600 | 1700 | 1800 | 1900 | 2000 |

MY **FAVORITE FLAVOR** IS STRAWBERRY!

Young kids don't always realize that they're supposed to spit out tooth-paste instead of swallowing it. Dental hygiene became less harrowing for parents in 1987 with the creation of safe-to-swallow toothpaste. But it wasn't invented for kids—it was made for astronauts so they could brush their teeth without having to spit in zero gravity.

1987
Space Spin-Off

CHAPTER 9

Holidays & Traditions

Have you ever stopped to think about some time-honored traditions and why we keep them? Take Christmas rituals, for example. Some might argue that dragging a giant pine tree into one's house each year and adorning it with sparkly stuff is a little odd. So why have people done it for centuries? Why do people wear green on St. Patrick's Day, or play pranks on April 1? These holidays and traditions are steeped in history—and surprises.

ST. PATRICK'S DAY

It's Not Easy **Being Green**

I t's a celebration of leprechauns, corned beef, and most of all, the Irish. But if you've ever been pinched for forgetting to wear green, you might have stopped to wonder: Where did this strange holiday come from?

It all started on March 17, 1631, when the Catholic Church decided to get around to honoring the patron saint of Ireland, St. Patrick. They were a little belated: He had died 12 centuries earlier. In that time, legends and lore about his life had piled up. One story says he drove all the snakes in Ireland into the sea—explaining why to this day, no snakes live there.

But the true tale of St. Patrick is even stranger than the fiction. Patrick was born in Britain, but at age 16, he was captured by pirates and sold into slavery in Ireland.

ST. PATRICK

After six years, he managed to escape and made his way back to Britain. Then he had a dream that showed him his destiny: to travel back to Ireland and become a missionary. He did, and spent the rest of his life converting people to Christianity.

IRISH FLAG

Bet You Didn't Know

The city of Chicago has been proudly dyeing its river green since 1962. It takes 40 tons (36 t) of dye to get the right shade.

It wasn't until 1798 that St. Patrick's Day got its green hue. Before then, the official color of the holiday was blue. But when the Irish rose up against British rule in the Irish Rebellion, they wore shades of emerald and sang a song about their repression called "The Wearing of the Green" as they went into battle. Green became part of St. Patrick's Day from then on. Today, it's not just the Irish who celebrate. People all around the world sport shamrocks, down green drinks, and, of course, don green clothing in St. Patrick's honor.

APRIL FOOLS' DAY

Got You!

HEH HEH, **FOOLED YOU,** SILLY PUP!

Switching sugar for salt. Sneaking food coloring into the milk. Putting plastic wrap on the toilet seat. If you needed some new ideas for your next April Fools' Day pranks, *you're welcome*. But why do we play tricks on the first of April?

The most popular theory says that the first April Fools' Day took place in the 1500s. During this century, the Western world had been following the Julian calendar (which began years on March 25 and celebrated the New Year a week later on April 1), but then it was discovered that the length of a year had been miscalculated by 11 minutes. Whoops!

To fix the mistake, the Western world changed to the Gregorian calendar (which started years on January 1). Some people were slow to get used to the switch—and pranksters took advantage of anyone who continued to celebrate the New Year on April 1. People would drop in on their neighbors to wish them a happy New Year and give each other silly presents. Anyone who was successfully tricked was an "April fool."

In 18th-century Scotland, April Fools' was a two-day celebration. On the first day, people tried to trick others into running made-up errands. Then came Tailie Day, which was all about playing pranks on people's rear ends: like pinning tails on them.

OMIGOSH!

In modern times, the media has gotten in on the joke. On April 1, 1957, the BBC reported that farmers in Switzerland were experiencing a record spaghetti harvest. Its video footage of people harvesting noodles from trees fooled many viewers. In 1998, Burger King advertised a Left-Handed Whopper that filled drive-throughs with duped customers. So the next time the holiday rolls around, be on your guard!

Bet You **Didn't Know**

On April 1, 2011, Swedish furniture chain Ikea promoted a new product: the Hundstol, a high chair for dogs. Ikea claimed it came complete with a hole in the back for the tail.

CINCO DE MAYO

¡Viva México!

Every year on May 5, people gather to march in parades, make speeches, and of course, eat lots of tacos. It's a big fiesta to celebrate Mexican Independence Day ... right? Wrong. Mexico's Independence Day is observed on September 16. So what are revelers celebrating on Cinco de Mayo?

Bet You Didn't Know

More than 81 million avocados are consumed in the United States on Cinco de Mayo. That's a lot of guacamole!

It all started in the early 1860s, when a series of wars had left Mexico in deep debt to several European countries. Mexican president Benito Juárez announced that he didn't have the funds to pay up, and French emperor Napoleon III got upset. He sent troops to get back the money and take over Mexico while they were at it. On their way to the capital, French soldiers passed through the town of Puebla—but that's as far as they got. Two thousand Mexican militia members were waiting for the 6,000 French soldiers.

It was a David-and-Goliath-style battle, and Mexico conquered the giant. The date? May 5, 1862.

The success was short-lived: The French regrouped, called for backup, and won possession of Mexico. But during their country's occupation, Mexicans chanted *"Cinco de Mayo!"* and celebrated their May 5 battle with food, songs, and dance to keep their spirits up.

Cinco de Mayo didn't become a well-known holiday until the 1970s, when American companies started marketing it as a new opportunity to sell party products. Today, Cinco de Mayo is a celebration of Mexican culture and heritage across America—but for Mexicans, the true day for celebrating freedom is September 16, the anniversary of the start of the Mexican War for Independence in 1810.

FIREWORKS

From **Bamboo** to **Boom!**

Sparklers, rockets, and firecrackers exploding in the sky are a traditional part of celebrations all over the world. But fireworks were actually invented in China, where people thought of them as a way to frighten off evil spirits.

During the Dong Han dynasty, which lasted from 206 to 220 B.C., people created fire-works by roasting bamboo over fires. Bamboo stalks are hollow and seg-mented, which make them flexible in nature. But when the stalks are held over flames, the air trapped inside each segment heats up and expands until the bamboo explodes with a *crack!*

Bamboo really exploded onto the scene about a thousand years ago when someone in China got the bright idea to combine saltpeter and sulfur (two chemicals used to make fires hotter) with flammable charcoal. That created an explosive substance that people started stuffing into bamboo. Expanding gases would shoot the flammable flora high into the sky: the first rockets. It wasn't long before the Chinese military modified the concoction for use in warfare. Today, we call it gunpowder.

When it wasn't being used for battle, the explosive powder made impressive fireworks, which quickly became an important part of celebrations in China, India, Persia, Europe, and eventually America. They've been as essential to America's Independence Day as hot dogs and parades since 1776. Then, Founding Father John Adams called for fireworks to light up the skies from coast to coast to celebrate the United States' new status as a free country.

NOOO!

IT'S **LIT.**

JOHN ADAMS, 2ND PRESIDENT OF THE U.S.A.

DIWALI

The Hindu **Festival** of Lights

Diwali is India's biggest and most important holiday. In October or November each year, millions of Hindus, Sikhs, and Buddhists from around the world come together for a five-day celebration.

Diwali, sometimes called Deepavalil or Dipawali, means "rows of lights." People use lamps and lanterns to decorate their homes and public spaces. Fireworks fill the skies. The light symbolizes the victory of good over evil. People in different parts of India have different beliefs about the origins of the holiday. In southern India, people celebrate it as the day the Hindu god Krishna defeated a demon. In western India, it marks the day another god, Vishnu, sent the demon king Bali to rule the underworld.

Each of Diwali's five days has its own set of traditions. The first day is considered a lucky day for shopping and cleaning the house. On the second day, people decorate their homes. On the third day, families come together to feast and celebrate. The fourth is for exchanging gifts. On the last day of Diwali, brothers visit their married sisters, who welcome them with a meal.

Today, setting off fireworks with a hiss and pop is Diwali's biggest tradition. But it's a new addition to this otherwise ancient holiday. Until the 1900s, pyrotechnics were so expensive they were for royals only.

Bet You **Didn't Know**

Some people believe that the sound of Diwali fireworks sends a message to the gods about the joy of people on Earth.

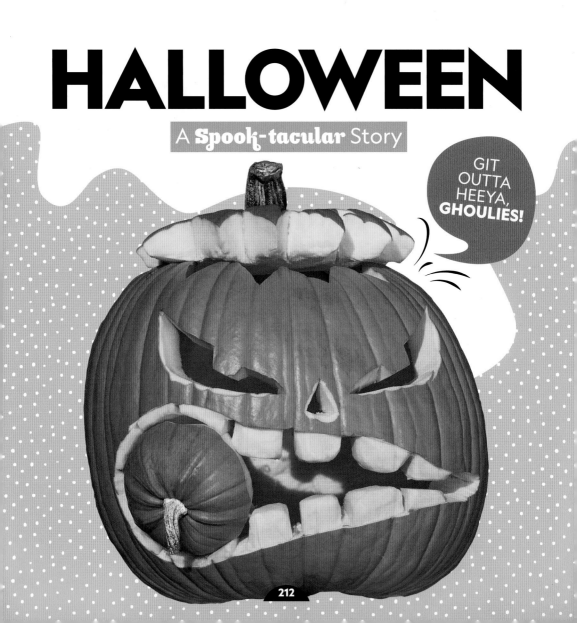

HALLOWEEN

A **Spook-tacular** Story

GIT OUTTA HEEYA, **GHOULIES!**

Nowadays, Halloween is a night for all kinds of frightful fun. You might carve spooky faces into pumpkins, dress up in a creepy costume, or collect basketfuls of candy. People have celebrated Halloween for more than 2,000 years—but it was sometimes more chilling than cheerful.

Halloween's roots lie in the ancient festival of Samhain, celebrated by the Celts, a group of people who lived in what is now Ireland, the United Kingdom, and northern France 2,000 years ago. They believed that on October 31, the living and the dead walked the earth together—and not all the spirits were good. Some thought evil ghosts caused trouble and damaged crops. To drive them away, the Celts would don animal skins and dress up as demons and goblins. They also carved faces into vegetables like turnips and potatoes—and pumpkins—and put them in their windows to scare off evil spirits.

The Celts believed that these spirits made it easier for their priests, called Druids, to predict the future. The Druids would sacrifice animals, then read fortunes in the burned remains. After that, families would light torches from the bonfire and use them to rekindle their home fires to help protect them during the coming winter.

By A.D. 43, the Romans had conquered most Celtic territories and banned sacrifices. But they kept Halloween, replacing the ancient Samhain festival with All Saints' Day, also called All Hallows, on November 1. The night before became All Hallows' Eve, eventually shortened to Halloween.

What's in **a Name?**

What do you call the night before Halloween? It goes by different names in different parts of America, including mischief night, trick night, and, strangely, cabbage night.

Strange SUPERSTITIONS

TREMBLE BEFORE ME!

Ancient people lived in an unpredictable, not-yet-understood world. Sickness could strike at any moment; the weather could bring a bounty or destroy the food they needed to survive. Superstitions gave people of the past a way to explain the unexplainable—and many of them still stick around.

The Number 13

So many people are scared of the number 13 that the fear has a name: triskaidekaphobia. It started with an ancient Norse, or Scandinavian, myth. According to the tale, 12 gods were invited to dine at the divine city of Valhalla. But one uninvited guest showed up: Loki, the god of mischief and discord. The myth was adopted by Christianity: In the story of the Last Supper, Judas, the disciple who betrays Jesus, is the last to join the table.

Black Cats

If a black cat crossed your path in the Middle Ages, you had a real problem on your hands: People in many parts of Europe thought that black cats were familiars, or the animal sidekicks of witches. But it wasn't always so. In ancient Egypt, cats of all colors were worshipped, and you were considered lucky if one crossed your path.

Walking Under a Ladder

This superstition got its start 5,000 years ago in ancient Egypt. A ladder resting against a wall forms a triangle. The Egyptians considered this a sacred shape that represented the gods, and they thought that walking through one dishonored them. The symbol was so important that they designed their greatest monuments—the pyramids—in triangles.

WHOOPS!

Broken Mirror

Break a mirror, the myth warns, and you'll be cursed with seven years of bad luck. Many cultures have been suspicious of mirrors, believing they could trap the soul of the person who peered into them. The ancient Romans thought if the mirror was broken, the soul would be broken, too. To reverse the curse, they ground broken mirrors into dust.

CHRISTMAS

A **Holly Jolly** Holiday?

Every year on December 24, children around the world eagerly wait for Santa Claus to slide down the chimney toting a sack full of presents. But it might shock you to learn that in the past, people were actually scared of Santa. That didn't stop them from celebrating the winter season, though—Christmas has its roots in traditions that have been going on for thousands of years.

In the time before electricity, winter was long, cold, and dark. The winter solstice, the shortest day of the year, was a time for celebration because it meant the days would begin getting lighter and warmer. In ancient Rome, people observed the winter solstice with a month-long party called Saturnalia. In Scandinavia, the Norse burned enormous logs for as long as 12 days. Experts now think that may be the origin of the Twelve Days of Christmas tradition.

HMM, WHO'S **BEEN NICE?**

Historians think that Santa Claus originated in ancient Germany. There, people believed that the god Oden took flight on midwinter nights—just like the modern Santa Claus. But unlike Santa, Oden wasn't exactly jolly: The Germans believed that he chose who would not live to see the next midwinter celebration. Many were so terrified of Oden that they spent the season hiding indoors! Merry Christmas?

When Christianity began to spread into Europe in the first centuries A.D., Christians adopted many old pagan traditions for their own midwinter celebration. The date of Christmas (December 25), for example, is celebrated as the birthday of Jesus Christ, but it isn't actually mentioned in the Bible. Instead, it was set in the fourth century A.D. by Pope Julius I to merge the new holiday with the midwinter festivals that people had been celebrating for thousands of years.

KWANZAA

Celebration of **Culture**

They place symbolic objects on a table, like ears of corn representing future generations. On the last day of Kwanzaa, everyone sits down for an African feast, called a Karamu.

Kwanzaa was officially established in 1966, during the civil rights movement in America. It was a response to the Watts riots in Los Angeles, which took place over six days in the summer of 1965 when racial tensions violently erupted. Now a professor of black studies at California State University, Long Beach, Maulana Karenga created the holiday to help bring people of African heritage together. The traditional colors of Kwanzaa reflect its message of unity: black for the people, red for the blood they share, and green for the rich land of Africa.

Some people might be sad on the day after Christmas, but for those who celebrate Kwanzaa, it means a new holiday has started. Beginning on December 26 and lasting for seven nights, Kwanzaa reconnects African Americans with their heritage. But there's more to the story of this holiday.

Kwanzaa means "first fruits," and the celebration began as a way to mark the harvest season. For thousands of years—since as far back as ancient Egypt—African cultures have been celebrating the yearly bounty of fruits and vegetables.

Though Kwanzaa has its roots in ancient celebrations, the modern version focuses on uniting people of African heritage. On each of the seven nights of Kwanzaa, families gather together. They drink from a cup called the Kikombe Cha Umoja, or Unity Cup, then pour out the last bit of liquid in honor of their ancestors.

BABY NAMES

What Did You **Call Me?**

New parents in the United States are allowed to name their baby just about anything. Celebrities have gotten especially creative: Cricket, North, and Denim are some of the more inventive monikers they've scribbled on recent birth certificates. But in other parts of the world, baby naming has strict rules.

For many cultures, naming a baby occurs during an important ceremony that marks an infant's entrance into the world. In Cambodia, where Buddhist people believe everyone is reborn into multiple lives, parents tie red string around their baby's arm to keep the mothers it had in past lives from visiting. Hindu people welcome a new child by putting honey in his or her mouth and whispering the name of God into the baby's ear.

Many parents turn to their religion for naming inspiration. In America during the 16th and 17th centuries, Puritans often named their children after virtues, or morals, like Prudence, Patience, and Mercy. Today, names that honor Islamic prophets, such as Mohammed, are common in Arab countries. In China, many parents closely consider family tradition and the baby's birth date. There are so many factors to think about that it's often weeks after the baby is born that they settle on a name.

In some countries, laws prevent parents from getting too creative. In Denmark, Iceland, and Germany, governments deny new baby names they deem too silly. Monkey, Pluto, and Stompie are all names that didn't make the cut. Perhaps they seem odd now, but as naming traditions change in the future, they might not seem strange at all.

YOU TALKING TO ME?

Bet You **Didn't Know**

Sometimes, Chinese babies are given "milk names," believed to ward off evil spirits until the child is strong and healthy enough for a permanent name.

Funerals THROUGH THE AGES

A LITTLE **MOISTURIZER,** PLEASE?

The way we grieve, lay our dead to rest, and remember them after they're gone varies from culture to culture. And over the millennia, funeral rituals have gone through big changes. Here are some of the most fascinating death rituals from the past.

3300 B.C.
Beloved Mummy

The first mummies were likely made by accident, the result of burying bodies in Egypt's hot desert sand until they dried out. Over many centuries, mummification became an art form. To make a mummy, ancient Egyptians would remove the dead person's organs and seal them in special jars. Then they would pack the body in salt for 40 days to dry it out. Finally, they would wrap the mummy in layers of linen. The more money the person's family spent, the nicer their mummy would look.

Timeline: 40,000 B.C. — 3500 — 3000 — 2000 — 1500

40,000 B.C.
Ancient Rites

We used to think of Neanderthals, an ancient cousin of modern-day humans, as slow-witted, knuckle-dragging cavemen. But now, scientists know Neanderthals were a sophisticated people who took care of their sick and even buried their dead. In 2016, archaeologists discovered the blackened remains of small ancient fires, each with a horn from an animal placed carefully inside. Scientists think the site is evidence that prehistoric people gave their dearly departed a ritual send-off.

1500 B.C.
Honoring the Past

About 3,500 years ago, the Chinese began a practice called ancestor worship. They believed that the spirits of the dead lived on forever and had the power to help or harm the living. To this day, some Chinese people perform rites to honor the spirits. They bury their dead in elaborate funerals and make offerings of food, flowers, and incense to the spirits at shrines in their homes.

350 B.C.
Going Out in Style

When King Mausolus, ruler of a bygone kingdom along the Mediterranean coast, died, he got one fabulous funeral: His broken-hearted wife, Artemisia, decided to build him a tomb worthy of their great love. The resulting structure, covered with carvings and decorated with statues, was so impressive that it was named one of the seven wonders of the ancient world. The ruins of the Mausoleum at Halicarnassus are in modern-day Turkey. To this day, bodies are still interred in "mausoleums," named in his honor.

210 B.C.
Army of the Dead

When Chinese emperor Qin Shi Huang Di died, he didn't want to go to the afterlife alone. So the emperor had one of history's most elaborate funerals: He was buried with a replica of his realm and an army of terra-cotta soldiers to guard it, each with unique facial expressions and carrying real weapons. The site was discovered in 1974, and archaeologists still haven't finished excavating it. They think there may be as many as 8,000 clay warriors, poised to protect their ruler.

| 1000 | 500 | A.D. 1 | 500 | 1000 |

A.D. 900
Ship Send-Off

As a nod to a life spent at sea, Vikings often buried their dead under ship-shaped burial mounds outlined with stone markers. But for monarchs and great warriors, a special kind of send-off was in order: the longship burial. The mightiest Vikings would be laid to rest in great wooden longships outfitted with everything they would need in the afterlife, like weapons. Sometimes the ships were buried; other times they were shot with a flaming arrow and burned at sea.

CHAPTER 10

Odds & Ends

A big part of what makes modern life modern is the quest of innovators around the world to turn wild ideas into real products that we use every day. Some of these incredible inventions have saved time; others have saved lives—but everything in this chapter has one thing in common: They had such odd starts, it's amazing they ever made it into your hands at all!

TU⋮⋮ERWA⋮E

Party **Plastic**

Nearly every household has some, often piled in a messy stack of tubs and lids that threatens to topple every time you open the cabinet. Today, there are all kinds of plastic food storage containers. But the pioneer was Tupperware.

Back in the 1940s, plastic was smelly, ugly, and shattered easily. No one had figured out what it might be good for—until an American man named Earl Tupper came along in 1946. Tupper, a chemist, discovered how to form plastic into flexible, durable cups and bowls with airtight lids to keep food fresh. It was a great invention—but Americans were still suspicious of plastics, and nobody bought it. Tupperware probably would have sat on the shelves forever if it wasn't for a woman named Brownie Wise.

Wise, a businesswoman living in Detroit, Michigan, U.S.A., saw Tupperware's potential.

She knew that in order for people to understand the product, they had to see it in action. So she pioneered selling Tupperware at "home parties," where she gathered her friends together to demonstrate and sell Tupperware. Wise dropped the bowls on the floor to show they wouldn't break and "burped" them to demonstrate how the seal let out air that would otherwise spoil the food.

TUPPERWARE PARTY IN 1963

Tupperware became trendy—and so did home parties, which later became known as Tupperware parties. Hosting Tupperware parties gave housewives a way to enter the workforce, become entrepreneurs, and make money for themselves. Wise started a network of Tupperware saleswomen across the United States that grew into an empire. In 1954, she became *Business Week* magazine's first cover woman, and her "party plan" model of selling is still going strong.

Bet You Didn't Know

Before Tupperware, people often used shower caps to cover dishes of leftovers.

GUM

A **Blown-Up** Tale

Blowing bubbles, sharing a stick with a friend, accidentally touching an ancient piece hidden under your school desk (gross!)—gum is a pretty common part of modern life.

But gum has actually been around for a long, long time. The ancient Maya and Aztec chewed on chicle, a sticky resin from the inside of the sapodilla tree that grows in southern Mexico and Central America. They used chicle to freshen their breath and clean their teeth, as well as to quench thirst and fight off hunger pangs. To them, chewing in public was socially unacceptable, so most people popped their chicle in private out of politeness.

In the 1850s, exiled Mexican president Antonio López de Santa Anna found himself in the United States. He wanted to return to power, so he decided to get rich by turning chicle into a substitute for rubber with the help of New York inventor Thomas Adams. Adams got stuck on the rubber project and it failed, but he realized chicle could make great chewing gum. It became gum's main ingredient until synthetic compounds replaced it in the mid-1900s.

Another person really turned gum into a gold mine: William Wrigley, Jr. In 1891, Wrigley, who worked as a soap salesman, decided to give free chewing gum to store owners who placed big orders. The gum gimmick proved a big success, so much so that Wrigley abandoned his soap sales. In 1893, he launched two of his own gum brands: Juicy Fruit and Wrigley's Spearmint. When he died in 1932, gum had made Wrigley one of the richest men in America. Chew on that!

DUCT TAPE

No **Quackery** Here

SURELY THAT'S A **TYPO?**

Have you ever been corrected for calling duct tape "duck tape"? Believe it or not, you weren't wrong! Originally, duct tape really was known as duck tape.

Back in the 1940s, when the United States was fighting World War II, the Army needed a way to keep boxes of ammunition dry during transport. Researchers at the manufacturing company Johnson & Johnson came up with a way to insert a type of cotton cloth called duck cloth between a smooth backing and a sticky adhesive. Soldiers called it duck tape because any moisture that hit the tape's backing slid off "like water off a duck's back."

I CAN BE YOUR **HERO!**

THE APOLLO 13 CAPSULE

After the war, people realized that the tape had all kinds of uses. Durable, water-proof, and very strong, it was perfect for fixing everything from broken windows to truck bumpers—and especially heating ducts. "Duck tape" became "duct tape." Soon, nearly everyone had a roll in the garage.

In 1970, duct tape earned hero status when it saved the lives of the three astro-nauts of the Apollo 13 moon mission. When one of their spacecraft's oxygen tanks exploded, the crew had to move to the small lunar module so they'd have enough power to get home. But there was a problem: The module only had enough oxygen for a crew of two. To survive, they had to figure out a way to connect a square device for scrubbing carbon dioxide from the air to a circular opening of the module's air filtration system.

NASA engineers hacked an adapter using space suit air hoses, tube socks, and yep—you guessed it—duct tape. The resourceful crew made it home safely—and now no U.S. space mission leaves Earth without a roll of the sticky stuff.

Bet You **Didn't Know**

Duct tape has been used to construct a working cannon, build a bridge, and lift a 500-pound (227-kg) car.

FIRE EXTINGUISHER

Stopping the **Flames**

As people began to cram into cities in the 17th century, one disaster became common: house fires. Flames could leap from home to home, demolishing entire neighborhoods in hours. Many people had to helplessly stand by and watch their belongings burn.

The first firefighting device was invented around 200 B.C., but it didn't work very well. It was basically just a big syringe filled with water that could be sprayed in the direction of flames. In medieval times, most people fought house fires with buckets of water or blankets to suffocate the flames.

In the late 1870s, several people invented "fire grenades"—glass globes filled with firefighting fluids, like water laced with salt to keep it from freezing. The idea was to hurl the globes at the flames so they would explode and the fluid within would put out the fire. One type had a chemical called carbon tetrachloride that extinguished flames. Unfortunately, it also created a gas, called phosgene, that turned out to be so deadly if inhaled it was used as a chemical weapon during World War I.

Bet You **Didn't Know**

The world's largest fire extinguisher is a Boeing 747 jet, modified to drop 20,000 gallons (75,700 L) of fire retardant across an area of land three miles (4.8 km) long.

All kinds of fire extinguisher designs were patented in the 19th and early 20th centuries. Most were based on the same simple idea: Cut off its source of oxygen and a fire will die. One extinguisher featured two tanks, one containing sodium bicarbonate (also known as baking soda) and the other filled with an acid. When the device was turned upside down, the contents of the tanks would mix and create a cloud of carbon dioxide that suffocated the fire. That basic two-tank design is still hot stuff today—it's what powers the red fire extinguisher many people keep at home for emergencies.

LIQUID **PAPER**

Mistake **Eraser**

RUH ROH

Nowadays, if you hit the wrong letter on the keyboard, you can simply tap the delete key to correct the error. But in the days of typewriters, a single typo meant starting all over. That changed in 1951, when one woman got creative and invented Liquid Paper.

Bette Nesmith Graham was a single mother in Dallas, Texas, U.S.A., who took a job as a secretary to support her son. The problem was that she wasn't a very good typist. Graham hated wasting time retyping documents after making small errors. She wondered: Since artists can paint over their mistakes on canvas, why couldn't I do the same?

Graham put some paint in a bottle and started dabbing it on her errors with a small paintbrush. Her boss didn't notice, but the other secretaries did. And they started asking Graham to share her secret. She began bottling her product, which she named Mistake Out.

Realizing she had a hit on her hands, Graham started the Mistake Out Company in 1956. She turned her kitchen into a laboratory and used her kitchen blender to mix up a better formula. Her son and his friends helped fill the bottles. Eventually, Graham made one too many typing errors. She was let go from her job, but she turned her misfortune into opportunity and devoted herself to her invention, then called Liquid Paper, full-time. By 1978, she was making 10,000 bottles a day.

Bet You **Didn't Know**

Graham sold her company in 1979 for almost $48 million.

WHAT'S IN THE **Junk Drawer?**

Unless you're unusually organized, you probably have one of these chaotic catchalls in your home. A junk drawer doesn't just contain a lot of handy items—it also holds their origin stories.

STICK WITH ME, KID.

Scissors

Leonardo da Vinci often gets credit for inventing scissors. But they actually date back to centuries before Leonardo was born. The ancient Egyptians had a version that looked like a long strip of metal with a blade on either end fashioned into a C-shaped curve. It remained the most popular scissor design for about 3,000 years.

Lint Roller

One evening in 1955, Nicholas McKay was getting dressed to chaperone a high school dance when he noticed—*uh-oh*—lint on his black suit. In a moment of inspiration, McKay grabbed an empty cardboard toilet paper roll, wrapped masking tape around it sticky-side out, and bent a wire hanger into a handle. The lint roller was born.

WE'RE PRACTICAL—
AND **RADICAL.**

Paper Clip

For as long as humans have been using sheets of paper, we've been looking for a way to keep them organized. It got much easier when a Norwegian inventor named Johan Vaaler patented the first paper clip in 1899. The useful little office supply once served as a symbol of protest when Nazi forces invaded Norway during World War II. The occupied Norwegians took to wearing paper clips on their clothes as a symbol of their country binding together.

I'M **NOT TACKY,** I'M ICONIC!

Pushpin

Throughout most of history, people used straight pins to hang their artistic masterpieces, battle plans, and maps on the wall. They also endured a lot of pricked fingers. It wasn't until 1900 that someone—a man named Edwin Moore from New Jersey, U.S.A., thought to put a handle on a pin for injury-free gripping. Moore made two dollars on his first sale. Now, pushpins are so iconic they're part of the collection of the Museum of Modern Art in New York City.

237

UMBRELLA

Got You **Covered**

When you reach for your trusty umbrella, it's probably because the weather forecast predicts rain. So you might be surprised to learn that the umbrella originated as a form of protection from the sun.

SUN, SUN, **GO AWAY!**

Umbrellas were invented more than 4,000 years ago, and there is evidence that people in ancient Egypt, Assyria, Greece, and China carried them. Early umbrellas were often reserved for the rich and powerful. In Persia, only the king was allowed to use one: It was made of linen and hung with long curtains to provide total shade and privacy. The Chinese were the first to realize that umbrellas could be used in the rain, too. They waterproofed their paper versions with layers of wax and lacquer.

What's in **a Name?**

"Umbrella" comes from the Latin word *umbra*, meaning "shade."

THANK GOODNESS FOR **NYLON!**

By the 16th century, umbrellas started popping open in the Western world. At first, only women carried them. English ladies covered the outsides of their umbrellas with feathers in the hopes that they would stay dry in the rain, like ducks. But it didn't work very well, so later, they swapped their plumage for oiled silk, canvas, or alpaca skin.

In the 1750s, an Englishman named Jonas Hanway finally got tired of being rained on. He pooh-poohed convention and started hoisting an umbrella on the streets of London. People mocked him, but by the time Hanway died in 1786, other men were carrying them, too. Today, umbrellas are acceptable for everyone, and come in collapsible, pocket-size, and even hat form.

NEON LIGHTS

The world would look a lot different at night without the brightly colored glow of neon lights. Just try to imagine Las Vegas or New York City's Times Square without them!

An incandescent lightbulb uses electricity to heat a thin filament until it glows. Neon light is different: It uses electricity to charge atoms so they glow. The first person to light upon this idea was a French astronomer named Jean Picard, who shook a mercury-filled barometer in 1675 and was shocked when it lit up. It wasn't until the 19th century that scientists figured out why: Shaking the mercury made static electricity that charged its atoms.

In 1898, two British chemists named William Ramsay and Morris Travers figured out how to separate a new element from air. The substance glowed bright red when charged with electricity. Ramsay and Travers named their discovery neon, after the Greek word *neos,* meaning "new." Other elements were found to glow when charged, too: Mercury vapor gives off blue light; carbon dioxide, white light; and helium, gold light.

There wasn't a use for neon—aside, hopefully, from scientists holding dance parties in their labs—until 1909, when a Frenchman named Georges Claude filled an airless glass tube with neon, zapped it with electricity, and created the world's first neon light. Two years later, he made the first ever neon sign, for a Paris hairdresser. People were awestruck by the new "liquid fire," and its popularity spread. Neon lights showed up in signs, storefronts, and dance halls. Now that's a bright idea!

Bet You **Didn't Know**

The O'Hare International Airport in Chicago, Illinois, U.S.A., has a one-mile (1.6-km)-long tunnel filled with 466 neon tubes.

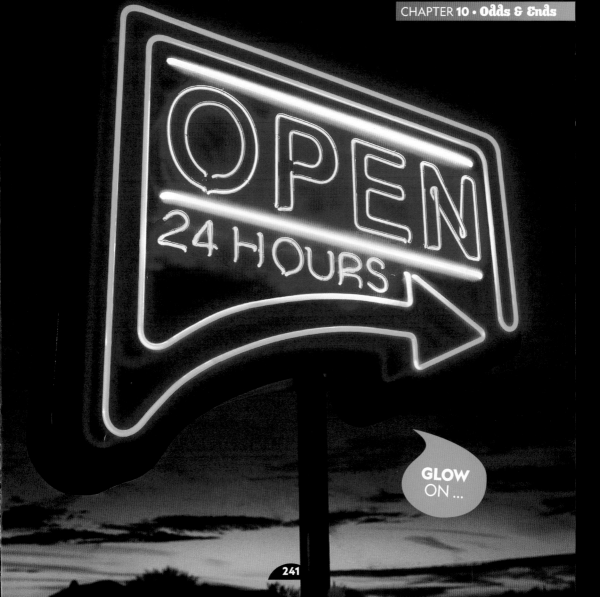

GLOW
ON ...

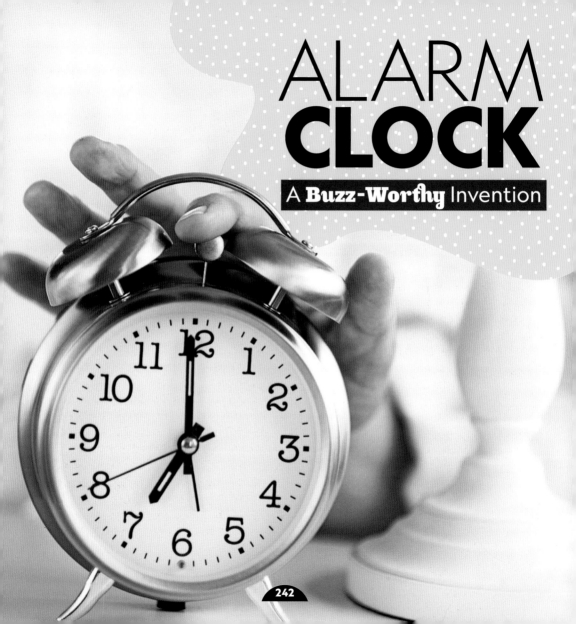

ALARM CLOCK

A **Buzz-Worthy** Invention

Beep, beep, beep! Ugh, your alarm, the most dreaded of all sounds. But before you slam your hand on the snooze button, think about how lucky you are that you don't have to endure the alarm clocks of yore.

The ancient Greek philosopher Plato was famous for starting his lectures at dawn. To make sure his students didn't miss them, he invented the first alarm clock, which he very considerately placed right next to the student rooms. Plato's clock used water dripping from one vessel into another to mark the passage of time. When the second vessel filled, it spilled a bowl of lead balls balanced on its top onto a copper platter—startling anyone within earshot awake. History doesn't say whether or not Plato was a very popular teacher.

RISE AND SHINE!

Bet You **Didn't Know**

Modern alarm clock inventions include one that wakes you up with the smell of cooking bacon and another that jumps off your nightstand and runs around the room until you catch it.

In A.D. 725, Yi Xing, who was a mathematician, engineer, astronomer, and Buddhist monk, used flowing water to turn the gears inside a clock. At set times, puppets would pop out and gongs would ring. By the 15th century, an unknown German inventor had shrunk down clock mechanics to create a personal alarm clock. It was a luxury item, though, so most people had to rely on church bells to wake up.

When the industrial revolution hit in the 18th century, people started to work in factories, and they had to be on time. Many used a service similar to a hotel wake-up call. They paid a "knocker-upper" to go from house to house, banging on doors or tapping on upper windows with a long pole to get them up. Suddenly, the blaring of your alarm doesn't seem so bad!

THE EARLY BIRD **GETS AN A!**

PLATO

Money THROUGH THE AGES

A t the beginning of civilization, people used to barter for goods they needed. A farmer might trade grain for milk or eggs for material to make clothing. Items traded have changed over the last 10,000 years. From shells to squirrel pelts, here are some of the oddest objects ever used as currency.

You can't eat a dollar bill when you're hungry. But the ancient Chinese thought it was smarter to create currency that could be used for more than just money. So they ground tea leaves and pressed them into bricks, which were used as a form of currency until the beginning of World War II. In some places, including Siberia and Tibet, tea bricks were favored over coins because they could be brewed or even eaten when food was scarce.

1200 B.C. Shelling Out

Cowrie shells, the outer bodies of small sea snails, were first used as currency in ancient China, and then in many different parts of the world. Small, easy to transport, and nearly impossible to counterfeit, they made perfect money. Many cowrie shells are the same shape and size, which meant payments could be weighed instead of counted one by one.

800 Edible Money

| 1200 B.C. | A.D. 1 | 300 | 600 | 900 |

A.D. 500 Selling Stones

In the middle of the Pacific Ocean, there's a tiny island called Yap where people have been using an unusual form of money for more than 1,500 years. There is no gold or silver on Yap, so ancient people decided the best candidate for money was the limestone on an island hundreds of miles away. They carved the limestone into huge stone disks and brought them back on bamboo boats to serve as currency. The pieces are so massive—some weighing more than a car—that they're only used for really big purchases.

1000
Fur Funds

Carrying around a bunch of squirrel pelts might seem totally bizarre. But that's exactly what people did in medieval Russia, where they were a common form of currency. The claws and snouts were even used as change. This strange system may have had an unexpected plus side: When the Black Death ravaged Europe, Russia was mostly spared. Rodents, including squirrels, carry the disease, and experts think the fact that their pelts had value might have helped keep Russia plague-free: People hunted rodents, which kept their numbers down.

THAT'S NUTS!

2007
Big Change

In 2007, the Canadian treasury released a coin worth a million dollars and made of pure gold. Don't worry, you couldn't lose it in the couch cushion: This coin is 21 inches (53 cm) across and weighs 220 pounds (100 kg). Even so, thieves managed to make off with one of the five coins in existence, stealing it from behind bulletproof glass at the Bode Museum in Berlin, Germany, in 2017.

| 1000 | 1900 | 1950 | 2000 | 2050 |

1950s
Gimme Some Cheddar

OK, it isn't actually cheddar—but one bank in Italy has been accepting cheese as collateral for loans since 1953! The system was designed to help the region's cheesemakers when times get tough. Credito Emiliano bank accepts wheels of Parmesan cheese as collateral—something of value pledged to a lender in exchange for a loan. The bank gives cheesemakers 34 months to pay back the loan—exactly the time it takes for Parmesan to age to cheesy perfection.

INDEX

Boldface indicates illustrations. If illustrations are included within a page span, the entire span is **boldface.**

PHOTO CREDITS

iStockphoto/GI; 93, Portrait of Galileo Galilei (1564-1642) (oil on canvas)/ Bridgeman Images; 94 (LE), Iwona Grodzka/SS; 94 (RT), Thawornnurak/SS; 95 (LE), Karlis Dambrans/SS; 95 (RT), Zeynep Demir/SS; 96, Gines Romero/SS; 97 (UP), Photo Melon/SS; 97 (LO), sjeacle/SS; 98 (UP), Tauleo/SS; 98 (LO), Jackan/SS; 99, Stocksnapper/SS; 100, The Image Bank/GI; 101 (UP), Patrick Faricy; 101 (LO), Rob Wilson/SS; 102 (UP), kaling2100/SS; 102 (LO), Georg Thellmann/SS; 103 (UP LE), iStockphoto; 103 (UP RT), Flynt/DRMS; 103 (LO), Jeffrey B. Banke/SS; **Chapter 5:** 104-105, MilanMarkovic78/SS; 105 (LO LE), WAYHOME studio/SS; 105 (LO CTR), Africa Studio/SS; 105 (RT), Africa Studio/SS; 106, eAlisa/SS; 107 (UP), Millenius/SS; 107 (LO), Frans Rombout/GI; 108 (UP), FLPA/Jurgen & Christine Sohns/GI; 108 (LO), Eric Isselee/SS; 109, Don Bayley/GI; 110, Sergio TB/SS; 111 (UP), LungLee/SS; 111 (CTR), Javier Brosch/SS; 111 (CTR), Susan Schmitz/SS; 112, Cris Foto/SS; 113, GI Europe/GI; 114, MilanMarkovic78/SS; 115 (UP), Jeremy Woodhouse 2008/GI; 115 (LO), Art Images/GI; 116 (LE), Robert Kneschke/SS; 116 (RT), Syda Productions/SS; 117 (UP), Dean Drobot/SS; 117 (LO), WAYHOME studio/SS; 118, Annette Shaff/SS; 119 (UP), FALKENSTEINFOTO/AL; 119 (LO), pryzmat/SS; 120 (UP LE), Madlen/SS; 120 (UP RT), Nikolich/SS; 120 (LO), Asmus Koefoed/SS; 121 (LE), Gilmanshin/SS; 121 (inset), studiovin/SS; 121 (RT), Philip Lange/SS; 122, Africa Studio/SS; 123 (UP), Richard Griffin/SS; 123 (LO), Zyankarlo/SS; 124 (UP), Wanchai Orsuk/SS; 124 (LO), Everett Historical/SS; 125 (LE), Capitano/SS; 125 (RT), TZIDO SUN/SS; 126 (UP), bitt24/SS; 126 (LO), A Roman Feast, (late 19th century) (oil on canvas) by Bompiani, Roberto (1821-1908)/Bridgeman Images; 127 (UP), Dja65/SS; 127 (LO), Tetra images RF/GI; **Chapter 6:** 128 (UP), nexus 7/SS; 128 (LE), Ron Zmiri/DRMS; 128 (LO CTR), 3DMI/SS; 129 (LE), Somchai Som/SS; 129 (LO LE), Bedroom of Diane De Poitiers in the Chateau De Chenonceau, Chenonceau, Indre-Et-Loire, France/Bridgeman Images; 129 (RT), MPanchenko/SS; 130, Anastasia Tcaci/SS; 131 (LE), Popovici Ioan/SS; 131 (RT), Hein Nouwens/SS; 132 (UP LE), Potapov Alexander/SS; 132 (LE), Pierre Choderlos de Laclos (1741-1803) (pastel on paper) by French School,(18th century); Musee de Picardie, Amiens, France/Bridgeman Images; 132 (RT), Somchai Som/SS; 133 (UP), The Print Collector/Heritage-Images/GI; 133 (LO), Edoma/SS; 134, M. Unal Ozmen/SS; 135, Ljupco Smokovski/SS; 136, Boris Sosnovyy/SS; 137, Rich Carey/SS; 138, iStockphoto; 139 (UP), Magneti-Marelli television receiver, 1938 Italy, 20th century/Bridgeman Images; 139 (LO), MPanchenko/SS; 140 (UP RT), Glowimages RF/GI; 140 (LO LE), Artmedia/Heritage Images/GI; 140 (LO RT), Hein Nouwens/SS; 140 (LO CTR), Shawn Hempel/SS; 140 (LO CTR RT), vvoe/SS; 141 (UP LE), iStockphoto/GI; 141 (UP RT), The Armada Portrait, c.1588 (oil on panel) by Gower, George (1540-96)/Bridgeman Images; 141 (LO RT), Thomas Crapper Toilets Plumbing Bathrooms Magazine, advert, UK, 1890s; The Advertising Archives/ Bridgeman Images; 142 (LE), Toxawww/DRMS; 142-143 (LO), Ljupco/DRMS; 142-143 (LO), photomaster/SS; 143 (UP RT), DeA Picture Library/The Granger Collection; 144, Monkey Business Images/SS; 145, Rolland Lynea/SS; 146, bumihills/SS; 147 (UP LE), 3DMI/SS; 147 (UP RT), Burachet/SS; 147 (CTR), Vereshchagin Dmitry/SS; 147 (LO), lynea/SS; 148, Ron Zmiri/DRMS; 149 (UP LE), Elena Elisseeva/SS; 149 (RT), Boyer/Roger Viollet/GI; 149 (LO), 2012 Michael R. Hicks/GI; 150 (RT), Luis Santos/ SS; 150 (LE), Bilanol/SS; 151 (UP RT), SingjaiStock/SS; 151 (CTR), David Papazian/SS; 151 (LO), Kunal Mehta/SS; **Chapter 7:** 152 (UP), Cal Sport Media/AL; 152 (LE), Michael Pettigrew/SS; 152 (LO RT), Daniel Milchev/GI; 153 (LE), Phumphao Sumrankong/SS; 153 (RT), Richard Paul Kane/SS; 154, Blend Images/GI; 155, Richard Paul Kane/SS; 156, Michael Pettigrew/SS; 157 (LE), aperturesound/SS; 157 (LO), Bruce Bennett/GI; 158 (LE), Igor Terekhov/SS; 158 (UP RT), Magdalena Wielobob/SS; 158 (LO RT), g-stockstudio/SS; 159, Rommel Canlas/SS; 160 (LE), Sergiy1975/SS; 160 (CTR), kimshanephotos/SS; 160 (RT), Phumphao Sumrankong/SS; 161 (UP), Bettmann Archive/GI; 161 (LO), NBAE/GI; 162, 2017 Adam Glanzman/GI; 163 (UP LE), Cal Sport Media/AL; 163 (LO), Paul Coartney/SS; 164 (UP), The Game of Pelota at Tula (mural) by Zalce, Alfredo (1908-2003)/Bridgeman Images; 164 (LO), Gladiators (gouache on paper) by Payne, Roger (b.1934)/Bridgeman Images; 165 (UP RT), Westend61/

Werner Lang/GI; 165 (CTR), Michael Nicholson/Corbi/GI; 165 (LO), Dragon Images/ SS; 166, Daniel Milchev/GI; 167 (UP), Chanwoot_Boonsuya/SS; 167 (LO), AFP/GI; 168, Photographer's Choice/GI; 169 (UP), WilleeCole Photography/SS; 169 (LO), courtesy Ultimate SwimFin; 170 (LE), Settawat Udom/SS; 170-171, Greg da Silva/SS; 172, aprilante/SS; 173 (UP), fStop/GI; 173 (LO), Aleynikov Pavel/SS; 174 (UP), The Image Bank/GI; 174 (LO), Icon Sportswire (A Division of XML Team Solutions)/GI; 175 (UP), Bettmann Archive/GI; 175 (LO), Judy Griesedieck/GI; **Chapter 8:** 176 (UP), Scisetti Alfio/SS; 176 (LO), Dundanim/SS; 176-177 (CTR), gresei/SS; 177 (RT), Africa Studio/SS; 177 (LO), espies/SS; 178 (LE), Scisetti Alfio/SS; 178 (CTR), PRISMA ARCHIVO/AL; 178 (LO), Danny Smythe/SS; 179 (UP), Michael Kraus/SS; 179 (LO), igorstevanovic/SS; 180 (LE), Vangert/SS; 180 (RT), quadshock/SS; 181 (UP), NatUlrich/SS; 181 (LO), DeAgostini/GI; 182, espies/SS; 183 (LE), Patrick Faricy; 183 (RT), Y Photo Studio/SS; 184, Yulia YasPe/SS; 185 (UP), Jeremy Red/SS; 185 (LO), traveler1116/GI; 186, ponsulak/SS; 187 (UP), Ruslan Murtazin/SS; 187 (LO), Holger Mette/GI; 188 (UP), ziviani/SS; 188 (LO), scyther5/SS; 189 (LE), Amawasri Pakdara/SS; 189 (RT), Thomaspajot/DRMS; 190, Africa Studio/SS; 191 (LE), Aedka Studio/SS; 191 (RT), Corbis NX/GI; 192 (UP), Archive Photos Creative/GI; 192 (LO), robert8/SS; 193, Damir Khabirov/SS; 194 (LE), Maks Narodenko/SS; 194 (RT), Stefan Wolny/SS; 195 (LE), Davydenko Yuliia/SS; 195 (RT), Jesus Cervantes/SS; 196, Villiers Steyn/SS; 197 (LE), Mile Atanasov/SS; 197 (RT), The Advertising Archives/AL; 198 (UP), Volodymyr Burdiak/SS; 198 (LO), Hayati Kayhan/SS; 199 (UP LE), kzww/SS; 199 (RT), Africa Studio/SS; 199 (LO LE), Andrey Armyagov/SS; 200 (LE), Kenneth Sponsler/ iStockphoto; **Chapter 9:** 200 (RT), Maya Kruchankova/SS; 200-201, Digital Vision/ GI; 201 (UP RT), Pikoso.kz/SS; 201 (LO RT), Hilary Andrews; 202 (LE), black-board1965/SS; 202 (RT), SuperStock RM/GI; 203 (LE), Jiri Flogel/SS; 203 (RT), Steve Geer/GI; 204, Ermolaev Alexander/SS; 205 (UP), Eric Isselee/SS; 205 (LO), Scott Rothstein/SS; 206 (LE), movit/SS; 206 (RT), Africa Studio/SS; 207, Steve Skjold/AL; 208 (UP), Kenneth Sponsler/SS; 208 (LO), ajt/SS; 209 (LE), somchaij/SS; 209 (RT), Everett - Art/SS; 210 (LE), espies/SS; 210 (RT), phive/SS; 211, Subir Basak/GI; 212, Klaus Kaulitzki/SS; 213 (UP), timquo/SS; 213 (LO), Hari Mahidhar/SS; 214 (LE), Ildo Frazao/GI; 214 (RT), Hilary Andrews; 215 (LE), Luisa Leal Photography/SS; 215 (RT), Corbis RM/GI; 216 (LE), LiskaM/SS; 216 (RT), Ivonne Wierink/SS; 217, Africa Studio/ SS; 218, Digital Vision/GI; 219 (UP), monticello/SS; 219 (LO), Image Source/AL; 220 (LE), Seregam/SS; 220 (RT), Sompong Tokrajang/SS; 221, Mike Watson Images Limited/GI; 222, DeAgostini/GI; 223 (UP LE), The Mausoleum at Halicarnassus by English School,(20th century); Private Collection/Bridgeman Images; 223 (UP RT), Tappasan Phurisam/SS; 223 (LO), Joe Scarnici/GI; **Chapter 10:** 224 (LE), Jens Molin/SS; 224 (RT), Corbis RF/GI; 224-225, tale/SS; 225 (UP RT), Roos Koole/GI; 225 (LO RT), Elena Elisseeva/SS; 226, absolutimages/SS; 227 (UP), SSPL/NMeM/Daily Herald Archive/GI; 227 (LO), eNJoy iStyle/SS; 228 (LE), CWIS/SS; 228 (RT), Javier Brosch/SS; 229 (LE), Wrigleys Magazine, advert, UK, 1950s; (add.info.: Food); The Advertising Archives/Bridgeman Images; 229 (RT), Roos Koole/GI; 230 (UP), Martin Good/SS; 230 (CTR), Brent Hofacker/SS; 230 (LO), Aksenova Natalya/SS; 231 (LE), Photo Melon/SS; 231 (RT), Edwin Verin/SS; 232, Mikhail Bakunovich/SS; 233 (LE), Jens Molin/SS; 233 (RT), Chones/SS; 234, Corbis RF/GI; 235 (UP), DutchScenery/SS; 235 (LO), elisekurenbina/SS; 236 (UP), BW Folsom/SS; 236 (LO), MNI/SS; 237 (UP), Ernie Janes/SS; 237 (LO), exopixel/SS; 238, A relief on a doorway of the hall of the Hundred columns depicting the king with two attendants, one of whom carries an umbrella/Bridgeman Images; 239 (UP), tale/SS; 239 (LO), Nadia Kompan/SS; 240, George Rose/GI; 241, Glow RM/GI; 242, Tetra images RF/GI; 243 (UP), jabiru/ SS; 243 (LO), Nice_Media_PRODUCTION/SS; 244 (UP), Sarymsakov Andrey/SS; 244 (LO), Wolfgang Kaehler/LightRocket/GI; 245 (UP LE), seawhisper/SS; 245 (UP RT), Andrea Bellemare/AFP/GI; 245 (LO), Rostislav Glinsky/SS; **Back matter:** 255, Gail Shumway/GI

For Mom and Dad, my most enthusiastic readers —SWD

Since 1888, the National Geographic Society has funded more than 12,000 research, exploration, and preservation projects around the world. The Society receives funds from National Geographic Partners, LLC, funded in part by your purchase. A portion of the proceeds from this book supports this vital work. To learn more, visit natgeo.com/info.

NATIONAL GEOGRAPHIC and Yellow Border Design are trademarks of the National Geographic Society, used under license.

For more information, visit nationalgeographic.com, call 1-800-647-5463, or write to the following address:
National Geographic Partners
1145 17th Street N.W.
Washington, D.C. 20036-4688 U.S.A.

Visit us online at nationalgeographic.com/books

For librarians and teachers: ngchildrensbooks.org

More for kids from National Geographic:
natgeokids.com

National Geographic Kids magazine inspires children to explore their world with fun yet educational articles on animals, science, nature, and more. Using fresh storytelling and amazing photography, Nat Geo Kids shows kids ages 6 to 14 the fascinating truth about the world—and why they should care.
kids.nationalgeographic.com/subscribe

For information about special discounts for bulk purchases, please contact National Geographic Books Special Sales: specialsales@natgeo.com

For rights or permissions inquiries, please contact National Geographic Books Subsidiary Rights: bookrights@natgeo.com

Designed by Sanjida Rashid

The publisher would like to thank everyone who made this book possible: Ariane Szu-Tu, editor; Catherine Frank, project editor; Shannon Hibberd, senior photo editor; Hillary Leo, photo editor; Alix Inchausti, production editor; Gus Tello and Anne LeongSon, design production assistants; and Scott Vehstedt, fact-checker.

Trade paperback ISBN: 978-1-4263-3529-7
Reinforced library binding ISBN: 978-1-4263-3530-3

Printed in China
19/PPS/1

MORE SURPRISES!

Now discover the science and engineering behind how stuff works in this cool series.